PICTORIAL PHOTOGRAPHY IN BRITAIN 1900-1920

4 May–11 June 1978 Hayward Gallery, London
26 July–19 August 1978 Midland Group, Nottingham
26 August–24 September 1978 Spectro Arts Workshop, Newcastle
6 October–1 November 1978 City Polytechnic, Sheffield
11 November–10 December 1978 Cliffe Castle, Keighley
16 December 1978–20 January 1979 Billingham Art Gallery
27 January–24 February 1979 Guildford House Gallery
3 March–1 April 1979 Royal Albert Memorial Museum, Exeter
11 April–5 May 1979 Gardner Centre Gallery, Brighton
12 May–10 June 1979 Scottish Arts Council Gallery, Edinburgh

Cover photograph: A. L. Coburn *Wapping* 1908

© Arts Council of Great Britain 1978
Essay © John Taylor
Catalogue designed by Lloyd Northover Limited, London
Catalogue edited and produced by Barry Lane, Photography Officer
Edition of 4,500 copies printed in duotone
by Shenval Press Limited, England
ISBN 0 7287 0171 5 softcover
ISBN 0 7287 0170 7 hardcover

A list of Arts Council publications, including
all exhibition catalogues in print can be
obtained from the Publications Department,
Arts Council of Great Britain,
105 Piccadilly, London W1V 0AU.

PICTORIAL PHOTOGRAPHY IN BRITAIN 1900-1920

Arts Council of Great Britain
in association with The Royal Photographic Society
1978

ACKNOWLEDGEMENTS

I should like to thank all those who helped in preparing this exhibition: in particular, Carolyn Bloore; Barry Lane; my colleagues Geoffrey Holt, John Myers, and Michael Vaughan (Stourbridge College of Art); Paul Lewis (Wolverhampton Polytechnic); Kenneth Warr, Valerie Lloyd, and staff of The Royal Photographic Society. I should also like to thank Russ Anderson; John Annan (T. and R. Annan and Sons Ltd); Edwin Appleton (The London Salon); Mrs E. Batkin; Dorothy Bohm (The Photographers Gallery); H. T. Bolus (Birmingham Photographic Society); Brian Coe (Kodak Museum); J. H. Cook; P. Doggett (The Camera Club, London); J. Donlevy and J. Haig (Yorkshire Photographic Union); Margaret F. Harker; R. Hershkowitz; Martin Hopkinson (Hunterian Museum, Glasgow); Ian Jeffrey; William Jenkins and Martha Jenks (IMP-GEH); Mr and Mrs T. Herbert Jones; Susan Kismaric (Museum of Modern Art, New York); G. Logan (Lancashire and Cheshire Photographic Union); Sandra Martin (Manchester City Art Gallery); R. Mason; Harry Milligan (North Western Museum of Science and Industry); Weston Naef (Metropolitan Museum, New York); Gael Newton (Art Gallery of New South Wales, Australia); Dr R. Nowak (Ilford Group); Colin Osman; Graham Ovenden; Leslie Penn (Birmingham Photographic Society); Terence Pepper (National Portrait Gallery); Joan Pollard; Oliver Green (The London Museum); Alexander Robertson (Leeds City Art Gallery); Aaron Scharf; Mrs M. Schlesinger; Robert A. Sobieszek (IMP-GEH); Hugh T. Stevenson (Glasgow Art Gallery and Museum); R. Tilling; Robin Vousden (The Whitworth Art Gallery); John Wall (National Photographic Record); Miss Joan Warburg, and the staff of Birmingham Central Reference Library, the Imperial War Museum, London, and the International Museum of Photography, George Eastman House, Rochester, New York (IMP-GEH).

John Taylor

CONTENTS

PREFACE

Previous historical exhibitions of photography mounted by the Arts Council, such as *'From Today Painting is Dead': the Beginnings of Photography* at the Victoria & Albert Museum in 1972 and *The Real Thing: an Anthology of British Photographs 1840 – 1950* at the Hayward Gallery in 1975, have been both large and broad in scope. The present exhibition has been conceived as the first in a series which will present in some depth the work of a particular period or theme in the history of British photography.

    Very special thanks are due to John Taylor who, assisted by Carolyn Bloore, has undertaken the main task of researching the period and selecting the photographs for the exhibition. We are greatly indebted to The Royal Photographic Society from whose collection the majority of the photographs have been drawn. Without the Society's generosity this exhibition, and an extended tour throughout Britain, would not have been possible. We would also like to express our gratitude to the many other lenders to the exhibition who are listed elsewhere in this catalogue.

Joanna Drew
Director of Art

FOREWORD

The achievements of British photographers in the 19th century are now relatively well-known, well documented and the works themselves frequently exhibited. By comparison the work of photographers from the first two decades of this century has remained largely unpublished and neglected.

Historians create history by their selective and deliberate use of evidence and their neglect of what is called 'pictorial photography' has been active and determined by a specific modernist approach. Indeed the term 'pictorial' is used more often as a term of condemnation rather than simple description.

The historian Helmut Gernsheim has described the photography of this period as 'a hybrid arising from a misconception of its functions' and continues 'when one art copies the characteristics of another decadence inevitably sets in'. Such phrases deserve close scrutiny since they condition our appreciation of the work.

By 1900 the advocates of photography as a fine art had already divided into two camps – the purists and the pictorialists. Both groups rejected the accumulation of fact through optical precision in favour of individual expression, but the purists thought it sufficient to obtain the perfect negative, whereas the pictorialists sought the beautiful and picturesque through various manipulative printmaking processes. Many of these processes such as gum bichromate, bromoil and carbon pigment processes were certainly hybrids, combining photographic reproduction with varying degrees of hand control over colour, tone and detail.

The resulting prints are frequently described as 'copying' or 'imitating' charcoal, chalk or wash drawings or conventional etchings and lithographs However it is usually forgotten that many of these photographers had been trained as painters and were simply extending the techniques at their disposal.

Since the recent flowering of similar 'hybrid' printmaking processes in the 1960s – photo silkscreen and offset lithography – the significance of 'purity' or truthfulness to function of separate techniques has become less relevant, and certainly less valid as a critical standard. Similarly Gernsheim's natural corollary that such hybrid forms would lead to decadence may be recognised as an unjustified assertion.

Recent photographic history has largely been written to illustrate the emergence and triumph of modernism. In Britain the period 1900 – 1920 was dominated by the debate between modernism and conservatism and the fact that the avantgarde was repulsed by the forces of conservatism has been sufficient to ensure that the Pictorialists have been suppressed or dismissed.

Thus traditionally it has appeared as if Alfred Stieglitz and the Photo-Secession of New York (founded in 1902), and especially Paul Strand's work published in the last issues of *Camerawork* in 1917, had anticipated the move towards abstraction and the new realism that took place in the 1920s. Against this progress pictorial photography in Britain has been judged worthy only of neglect.

At a time when other critics are challenging the hegemony of the modernist perspective John Taylor's essay and selection of works for this exhibition present a challenge to orthodox histories of the period. The exhibition demonstrates the strength of this period in British photography and the excellence of our contribution is set against Continental and American works, few of which have been seen here in recent years. Many pictorialists who have been completely neglected are introduced for reappraisal by a modern audience.

Barry Lane
Photography Officer

A. L. Coburn *Portrait of G. B. Shaw* 1908

PICTORIAL PHOTOGRAPHY IN BRITAIN 1900-1920

In nineteenth century France, those who expected tradition to curb the individual talent were met with demands from within the schools, and from the Salon des Refusés of 1863, to value originality and dispel the complacency of the *juste milieu*.[1] In his '*Salon*' of 1866, Zola wrote:

Fig.1 Robert Demachy *L'Effort*

'It is no longer a question here . . . of pleasing or not pleasing, it is a question of being oneself, of baring one's breast, of energetically forging one's individuality'.[2]

Originality had always been an estimable quality amongst 'official' Salon artists, but it was held to be insufficient in itself: the unique contribution of the individual should be tempered by the weight of the past. Painters who believed this continued to be honoured, but their achievements seem to be incomplete compared with the work of those artists who ignored the limits of convention.

The history of French painting in the late nineteenth century is by and large the history of a debate created by antagonistic minds. The arguments that occupied the French painters were rehearsed by photographers from 1890 to 1920 at least, and as in France the avant-garde has won acclaim. Alfred Stieglitz and some American Photo-Secessionists such as Clarence White, and Steichen, have enjoyed high reputations as avant-garde spirits, whereas others who also believed in the future of photography as a fine art have been relatively ignored, as if the propaganda of Stieglitz himself, and of Paul Strand, provided an assessment which could not be challenged.

But in Britain the power of convention dispelled the threat of avant-garde novelties. This has resulted in a regrettable neglect of the British contribution to photographic history, which has been regarded as being irrelevant to modernism, as if modernism and the method of its study were something other than local and historical circumstance.

This aspect of photographic history – the shift of the conventional frame of reference into an assured but increasingly irrelevant position – can be seen in the various schisms that took place amongst photographers in Britain.

THE SALONS

One significant break occurred in 1892 when members of The Royal Photographic Society broke away to form the Linked Ring Brotherhood, which organised the Photographic Salon from 1893 until 1909. The photographers who seceded felt that the 'Royal' was too bound up with the science and trade of photography to allow scope to the artistic pretensions of its members. Once these men had proclaimed that photography was a medium of individual expression they aligned themselves, quite consciously, with known aesthetic values, which acknowledged the importance of Nature, of truth to the medium, and of the personal vision. Conflict arose only in the balanced translation of these qualities into the final print. 'A typical example of control may be seen in the comparison of Demachy's silver chloride postcard of *L'Effort* (fig. 1) with the version in gum-bichromate (plate 7)'.

However, from 1902, when the Photo-Secessionists began exhibiting as a group, and American work was commonly seen in the Photographic Salon, they presented a challenge that quite disrupted the condition of photography in

Britain. The Photographic Salon of 1908 was deemed a failure because it excluded too many Links and included too much work by a clique that became known as 'The American Selecting Committee'.[3]

'English contributors have been ... either rejected altogether, or represented very badly, whilst the Americans are in more than usual strength. This becomes very significant when it is remembered that five Americans were on the hanging committee and still more significant is the fact that two of them are represented by thirty-nine and twenty-one works respectively.[4]

'So intense was the feeling ... that Mr. F. J. Mortimer, editor of the *Amateur Photographer*, hastened to the packers and succeeded in capturing the rejected pictures before they were returned to their owners. From them he selected 128 prints and organised what is known as the Photographic Salon des Refusés' ...[5]

The Salon des Refusés was a challenge both ideological and political, and was of considerable consequence. Ideologically, the exhibition represented a hardening of attitude against progressive British workers, such as Malcolm Arbuthnot, and against Americans in general, who were reputedly gulled by novelty, which could never be an aspect of pictorialism. Pictorialism treated of immutable Nature.

In 1908 the relationship that existed between British pictorialists and the Photo-Secessionists began to break up. The programme of the Little Gallery of the Photo-Secessionists published in December 1908 announced the winter exhibition of the 'New British School' (Messrs. Malcolm Arbuthnot, Walter Benington, E. Warner and others)', but this show never took place.[6] Whilst in London the Photo-Secessionists who were deemed to have ruined the Photographic Salon were excluded from the Salon des Refusés.

'no one will expect to find the American Style rampant here, with its calculated avoidance of the ordinary in pictorial matters'.[7]

A measure of the Salon des Refusés can be taken from the statement printed on the catalogue:

'The progress of art will not be advanced by startling innovations or by the endeavour to gain ephemeral notoriety by means unworthy of the artist's high vocation, but by the gradual and keener perception and expression of nature and beauty, apart from mere temporary art crazes and artistic shibboleths.'

The political consequence of Mortimer's action was to gain him a place on the Selection Committee for the Photographic Salon of 1909[8], and to ensure the exclusion of the prominent Americans Alvin Coburn, Frank Eugene, Joseph Keiley, Steichen, Stieglitz, Clarence White, and the Baron de Meyer, who had contributed 118 out of the 203 works in the 1908 Photographic Salon.[9]

It had already been suggested that the Photo-Secessionists would not appear again at the Photographic Salon.

'American pictorialists are inclined to deny the English school the right of any precedence of exhibition authority, and it is well within the bounds of probability that New York will oust it and keep the lead in the way of organising international exhibitions of pictorial work. Certainly, so far as America is concerned, the London Photographic Salon has quite lost whatever hold it once had upon the sympathies of the pictorialists. The latter have a feeling that they have been 'exploited' by certain persons in London, and are disinclined to submit to such undignified captivity any longer.[10]

This cast on events would have been incomprehensible to most of the British. Their concern was the preservation of a Salon in London for the exhibition of international pictorialism, and if the Photo-Secessionists were perceived to have excluded the Links on one occasion, the Links were determined that the intrusion should not recur. Unhappily, there was dissent amongst the Links, and this produced the second secession amongst British photographers. In 1910 the London Salon replaced the Photographic Salon of the Linked Ring.

The organisers of the London Salon stated quite simply that its object was 'to confine its exhibits to those pictures in which individual artistic aim and feeling have found their expression by means of the camera'. The majority of British contributors to the new Salon had earlier been selected by Mortimer for his Salon des Refusés. The important Links, Craig Annan, Arbuthnot, Benington, and Davison, who had served on the 1909 Selection Committee, and voted to suspend group activity in 1910 so that 'members or groups of members should be at liberty to act as they pleased'[11] were excluded. Baron de Meyer and Alvin Coburn, members of the controversial 1908 committee, held their own two-man show at the Goupil Galleries in the spring; Arbuthnot was arranging a one man show for the Vienna Camera Club, and all of them exhibited at Stieglitz' exhibition at the Albright Galleries in Buffalo (1910). Only Frederick Evans was included in the 1908 Salon, the Salon des Refusés, the 1909 Selection Committee, the London Salon, and the Buffalo exhibition, but then his reputation was extremely high: of the newcomers, Dudley Johnston was represented in exactly the same variety of exhibitions, except that he objected to the 1910 show and never exhibited work at the London Salon.

The schism amongst British photographers was accompanied by some acrimony, and the defeated Links looked for yet another 'secession' to counter the London Salon. Since Evans had aligned himself with the London Salon it was necessary to obtain the help of the other major British photographer of international repute, George Davison, a leader in the 1892 secession. Both Coburn and Arbuthnot wrote in June 1910 and urged him to participate in a new group show. Davison replied to Arburthnot:

'I see no reason why there should not be an exhibition at the New Dudley Gallery next September if the men whose work counts will support it. This need not drain them to such an extent that they could not also do still more for an exhibition in the Spring, and it would help keep the proper spirit alive.
In these matters it seems to me all must turn on what the workers will do for the show. If Annan, Steichen, de Meyer, Coburn, Stieglitz, yourself, Benington, and one or two others will send work, an interesting result is assured, and I shall be very pleased to co-operate whether I have anything new to send or not'.[12]

The exhibition was eventually organised in May 1911 at the Newman Gallery, and it was known as 'The London Secession.'

'The London Secession is a name intended to suggest the close parallel and sympathy with the American 'Photo-Secession', for some years now the leading organisation of pictorial photography in the world . . .[13]

The bitterness that had been aroused by the collapse of the 'Ring' was reported in *Photography and Focus*, edited by R. Child Bayley, who supported 'The London Secession'.

'It has been openly avowed by members of the 'Ring' that some of the latest recruits to that body were admitted for no other reason whatever than that it was hoped they would support it in the press! There could only be one end to such a policy, and it came swiftly. The 'Ring' collapsed. The less important members got up an exhibition in the autumn of last year under the title of the 'London Salon' from which almost every leading worker was absent . . .'[14]

Francis Mortimer, who was a founder member of the London Salon, had quite a different attitude to this secession, which he called a 'little exhibition' by a 'small coterie' of photographers. In his review Mortimer praised the frames and the gallery before the pictures, which were successful because they had been rigorously selected and were full of sunlight – 'principles we have been endeavouring to impress during the past year'.

'Incidentally, the exhibition has apparently been the means of resuscitation of more than one of the early workers in the Linked Ring whose pictorial productions have not been much in evidence in recent years. If the show has only been the means of bringing these back into activity again, it will at least have served a useful purpose'.[15]

Each photographer exhibited three works, and Mortimer remarked upon these at some length, but he just mentioned that Stieglitz and Annie Brigman had work on display, and this no doubt for a very particular reason.

Stieglitz had published two pamphlets in 1910 entitled 'Photo-Secessionism and its Opponents' which attacked rival American entrepreneurs such as Zimmerman and Fraprie, but was especially shrill in its condemnation of F. J. Mortimer. Mortimer had pirated some gravures of Annie Brigman's from *Camera Work*, and reproduced them in the *Amateur Photographer*.[16] Mrs. Brigman challenged him, and his answers were considered 'insult being added to the injury.'[17] Mortimer's editorial[18] served only to enrage Stieglitz further since the term 'self-seeker' which he had chosen to berate any jealous opponent, was turned on Stieglitz himself. Mortimer, too, had suffered some indignity. The first pamphlet had been sent to Child Bayley, who was his rival in editorial power. Mortimer had claimed that Bayley had told Stieglitz to mind his own business, but Bayley was quick to deny this. Stieglitz' second pamphlet of October 1910 was extremely abusive, but more significant than the almost hysterical tone is Stieglitz' determination to separate his Photo-Secessionist movement, which he considered artistic and progressive, from British pictorialism. Stieglitz accused Mortimer of being responsible, along with others, for 'a perilous situation' in photography.

'As I hold the future well-being of photography very dear I must see to it that those forces which militate against it be opposed and destroyed'.[19]

In fact, Stieglitz was attacking the 'philistine' in order to adopt a conspicuous avant-garde posture.

The London Salon exhibited the works of pictorialists who had fallen out with Stieglitz, particularly Rudolph Eickemeyer, and newcomers like Edward

Weston. Indeed up to 1916 there would seem to have been a sympathetic appreciation of the cultural differences between the U.S.A. and Britain. Although Mortimer himself may have been reluctant to endorse the more unnatural innovations, such as Coburn's Vorticist portraits of De Zayas and Ezra Pound, exhibited at the London Salon in 1916, he must take credit as editor of the *Amateur Photographer* for enabling the British public to take stock of the changing situation.

The London Salon continued as the major international exhibition of pictorial photography, whereas 'The London Secession' ceased to exist. No Photo-Secessionists exhibited in the London Salon save for Eugene and Kasebier in 1910 and Coburn in 1916. The Royal Photographic Society accepted an 'American Invitation Collection' of work by Photo-Secessionists, in 1914, but some of the best work had already been shown in London at the Photographic Salons.

After 1911 there were no upheavals in the organisation of British Salon photography, but the events of 1908-1911 had negated experiment as a true aspect of pictorialism. Although the catalogues of the London Salon from 1916-1920 stated that work should show 'distinct evidence of personal artistic feeling and execution' the phrase does not describe the situation. The tenor of the work is embodied in the terse celebration of Nature and Beauty in the catalogue of the Salon des Refusés. The irony of this Salon of retrenchment would not have been lost on Stieglitz, or anyone who had observed the French experience. Individual expression was important, but more important was restraint, or what was once understood as decorum. The defeat of avant-gardism and the strengthening of conventional attitudes were real forces in British cultural life, and as such require further investigation. The elucidation of attitudes that were commonly held should reveal the special contribution of British photographers.

AESTHETIC VALUES

If individual talent was in the last resort subordinate to tradition, the determining factor of the tradition should be understood. In his *Salon* of 1866, Zola made his famous statement 'a work of art is a corner of creation seen through a temperament', and this idea seems to have been important for H. Snowden Ward since he used it on more than one occasion.[20] It is the slight alteration of Zola's phrase and its interpretation that are revealing.

'Art is 'nature seen through a temperament'. Without observation, our art becomes a travesty of Nature . . .'[21]

Whilst imagination was required, and reflection was of consequence, neither signified if Nature was ignored.

The problem of definition, or reasonable deformation of nature, left many photographers and critics clinging to a system of rules of composition that was always too rigid. Although it was often stated that rules in art were only guidelines it became difficult to dismiss the precepts, or to see that both 'art' and 'nature' might not be quantities at all, or even elusive ideals, but exist only as conventions themselves, and thus be subject to radical change.

Nature was still closely associated with Truth and Beauty, and both of these abstractions had undergone some peculiar transformations during the course of the nineteenth century. No ground can be identified that was common to all

Fig.2 Eustace Calland *The Mall* 1896

THE CAB-STAND,
BY LLEWELLYN MORGAN.
With apologies to Mr. Eustace Calland.

Fig.3 from *Photograms of the Year* 1897

photographers: some thought that beauty and truth resided in nature itself, whilst others believed that this degree of order or value was lent to the world by the imagination. Quite clearly this last view was modern, but it was confused by belief in general truth, Platonic Beauty, and morality, and dressed in a contemporary style akin to Whistler's Nocturnes. Photographers adapted the forms of the art of the recent past to create a version of Aestheticism or 'art for art's sake' which was remote from the forms in the Fine Arts and in literature. Photographic aestheticism was remote not only because it was empty of decadence and neurosis, but because it was described almost entirely in the critical language proper to an earlier stage in the arts, when works such as 'breadth' 'tone' and 'aerial perspective' had been adequate or even powerful critical terms. The rules of composition had hardened by 1896, when Eustace Calland exhibited 'The Mall' (fig. 2). The reviewer insisted upon the 'good qualities' of this picture, achieved 'in spite of the violation of conventional rules and prescriptions'.[22] The amateur response was a 'pictorial parody' (fig. 3),[23] which indicated one conviction of the subject matter and treatment that might properly be called artistic.

Picture divided.   Still unsatisfactory.   Much better.

Fig.4 from *Photograms of the Year* 1902

In 1902 the situation was much the same for many practitioners who learned that certain conventional devices were to be used to avoid 'undesirable lines'. (fig. 4).[24] Between 1900 and 1920 many British photographers succeeded in creating a conspicuous style which was often stated in these obsolete terms. Indeed, one aspect of the absence of modernity in British pictorial photography rested in the amateur neglect of a policy towards the evolving new style, which suffered still under the careless application of irrelevant theory. The new style is quite easily seen in comparison with the British art still popular at the Royal Academy, which continued the anachronistic traditions of the art of the 1890s. The photography of the period was an elaboration of the photo-impressionism begun in the 1890s. But there was an unusual coincidence of technical fashions with the wide assimilation of notions of art unrelated to the earlier moral and anecdotal fables. In 1900 a reviewer said:

'On the walls of an average simple English home paintings by Birkett Foster, photographs like H. P. Robinson's, are fit and proper, and until recently the bulk of English art is rightly in keeping with the atmosphere of roast beef, and the conventional life of the wealthy bourgoisie. The appreciation of Whistler and the signs of his influence denote a change in taste and ideas.'[25]

Horsley Hinton was one of the pioneers of photographic impressionism, and in 1901 he was accused by Bernard Shaw of being a propagandist for the new 'fuzzographers', of whom Shaw disapproved.

'just as, fifteen years ago, Mr. Whistler, in order to force the public to look *at* and *for* certain qualities in his work, would draw a pretty girl and then obliterate her face by slashing his pencil backwards and forwards across it, in order to check-mate the 'Who is she?' and 'Ain't she pretty!' people; so does Horsley Hinton fail to satisfy in the transition from clear definition to downright blur'.[26]

The commentary and the photograph which mixed the effect of f32 with f3, for instance, were intermediary stages, in the evolution of a photographic art towards a decisive commitment to impressionism. In 1901, distinct and realised impressionistic photographs had been exhibited already in the Salons, and both Shaw and Hinton are symptoms of the cautious approach to anything that might be regarded as novelty – Shaw in his dislike of such work, and Hinton in his attempt to marry the styles in a manner 'too instructive'.

Since Beauty and Truth were the quest of the pictorialist, novelty was shunned. The pictorialists generally were not familiar with recent developments in art, and seem to have wished to preserve themselves against 'excess' and the 'Pushing a l'outrance of startling novelties'. In 1902 a critic of Steichen's work said:

'Most of us remember or have read of the pre-Raphaelite movement in England which did not amount to much more than a vigorous protest by the artists, thinkers, and workers in oil of that day, against slipshod drawing, carelessness, and want of definition.

The wave of pre-Raphaelitism soon subsided ... and gave place to impressionism, which has apparently gained a firmer and more lasting hold on the artistic world.

It is difficult now to realise how two such movements diametrically antagonistic as pre-Raphaelitism and impressionism could have flourished in the brief space of half a century, but they did, and one is still with us ... Although we must admit that photographers have for some time been sleeping the sleep of Rip van Winkle, when waking up in their tatters of pure photography and rubbing their eyes at modern innovations, let them not don the too brilliant and garish garments of the present fashion, which may lead them into paths where ridicule and contempt alone will wait their too revolutionary guise'.[27]

This sort of admonition against novelty was extremely common and was aimed most often at American photographers, but by 1902 the 'revolution' was complete and the impressionists were established in the Salons.

Bernard Shaw claimed that the 'cleverness and chic in gum' had confused the members of The Royal Photographic Society, who were uncertain of their role amongst the photographers who favoured the pigment processes. On the other hand the members of the Linked Ring Brotherhood were more active in the debate of photography as a fine art and did not shirk the latest developments.

'The Royal Photographic Society mixes up optics and fine art, trade and science in a way that occasionally upsets the critical digestion. It is divided between two quite incompatible interpretations of the word exhibition, which means sometimes a huge international display of industrial products, with gold medals for future use as advertisements, and sometimes a collection of works of fine art. To complete the muddle, The Royal Photographic Society has been so effectually laughed out of its old actions that photographs are to be esteemed according to certain technical conditions in the negative, that it has now arrived at the conclusion that a pictorial photograph is one in which the focussing and exposure

Fig.5 A. Horsley Hinton *Weeds and Rushes* 1902

are put wrong on purpose. Consequently, whilst it solemnly medals some of its exhibits as if they were sewing machines, it is afraid to give a medal to any picture which does not look more or less mildewed, lest it should be ridiculed for Philistinism.'[28]

In contrast the 'Photographic Salon' of the Linked Ring welcomed skillful work in the pigment and platinotype processes, although the purist Shaw much preferred the latter because pigment was 'much more controllable in the wrong direction'. By 1902 Shaw had approved the work of Horsley Hinton, who produced 'pure photography by great skill in negative making and painting', whereas the 'clever draughtsmen' manipulated 'the pigment processes so as to dissemble photography as much as possible'.[29]

Horsley Hinton used combination printing, but did not revert to the illustrated homily. In addition, his use of the platinotype process established distance between himself and the impressionists. He said that because no-one like Whistler, who could apparently produce works of art without effort, had yet been created among the photographers, they must continue to labour for their rewards, but the result need not be anecdotal. His exhibition print of 1902, 'Weeds and Rushes', (fig. 5) was made up of three negatives. The land itself was 'improved' – he pulled up a large dock plant and placed it on the left of the composition, but still in the best negative he did not much like the trees standing bare and so he added some clouds to suggest space beyond, and he added the ridge to 'suggest where perhaps this reed-grown stream finds its source'.[30]

Hinton did not want his photograph to be identical with the English landscape. He wanted the picture to conform with a notion of landscape apparently untidy in its details (for these have been retouched) but coherent as a whole. Since the photographer's fiction resembled the real world it was easy to blur the fiction altogether into a form of general truth.

Most pigment photographers would have regarded such a confection in platinum as no different in kind from their own work, and it seems that the arguments centred, and rested, upon the choice between the few degrees of control that were inevitable, and those indulgences (or creative acts) so beloved of the handworkers.

Frederick Evans was a purist, and he thought the choice of the platinum process was the one decision that would ensure truth to nature.

'One charm and advantage that a really artistic photograph of a cathedral interior has over a drawing or painting is that it is so evidently true to the original subject: one does not instinctively feel inclined to ask, how much of this effect is due to the particular vision or translation of the painter? Or how far is it not only a picture but also a true picture of a great building? There is an instant conviction about an artistic photograph of a cathedral interior; it appeals with an air of necessary truth to fact; and its equally important air of necessary truth to art should and may be equally in evidence.'[31]

The platinum salts were embedded in the paper; there was no emulsion, so the picture did not float above the paper, or shine, but there was no lack of light. Each delicate tone seemed to be suffused with light which actually belied the 'fact' of the cathedral interior, since this light existed only in the print. Removed as we are from the arguments for and against control, the platinotype seems equal in its capacity for compromising 'truth to fact' with the 'airs' of art to create a world every bit as remote as the inventions of the gummists.

The purists objected most strongly to the 'twilight school' of the hand-workers because they seemed to have eliminated light to produce what Evans called 'all-over alike, low toned, "treacly" things.' Whistler was to be dissociated from such effects. A. J. Anderson was very sceptical of these 'incessant nocturnes' and 'mid-day harvest scenes in a few tones of dingy brown', since 'Whistler would follow a nocturne with a bit of sparkling colour'.[32]

In 1878 Whistler had said 'The imitator is a poor kind of creature. If the man who paints only the face, or flower, or other surface he sees before him were an artist, the king of artists would be the photographer.'[33]

Commenting upon these remarks in 1904, Will Cadby remarked that it seemed 'nothing short of barbarism to mention in the same breath the gay butterfly and the prosaic camera.'

'But photography has changed since 1878 . . . It is now generally admitted that the lens is no longer *only* the king of imitators; and although (in 1878) few camera-workers could have found in Whistler's utterances on art much that they would have had the temerity to apply to their own craft, such is not the case now. Photographers have become bolder, and take their own work more seriously.'[34]

He then listed a few quotations to 'profitability ponder upon', and the first of these is of special significance.

'To say of a picture, as is often said in its praise, that it shows great and earnest labour, is to say that it is incomplete and unfit for view. Industry in Art is a necessity – not a virtue – and any evidence of the same, in the production, is a blemish, not a quality.'[35]

Evidence of 'great and earnest labour' was improper in Art and betrayed a lack of sensibility. Walter Pater said the intense experience of creation was suffered by the 'quickened multiplied consciousness'. To create Art one had not only to recognise the heightened moment, but to submit to its charms rather than industriously pursue them.

'Art comes to you, proposing frankly to give nothing but the highest quality to your moments as they pass, and simply for those moments sake'.[36]

This tenet of Aestheticism, made in 1873, would have seemed particularly attractive to the photographer. It had been claimed that individual expression was best achieved by being passive, so that Nature might continue to suggest the moments of Art. The photographer had often felt cheated of artistic status because so much of the *work* was nothing but a chemical reaction. Now the mechanical aspects of the photograph were an advantage because 'earnest labour' was considered inartistic. The active imagination had been transformed into a receptacle that was analogous to the camera itself: the photograph received and held the moment seen by the 'quickened multiplied consciousness'.

In 1873, 'Art for art's sake' was remote from the photographer since he was interested chiefly in 'fact' and the camera could provide an abundance of this. In 1904, when many more people were practising photography, when photography was the relaxation of men whose training in art was either negligible or incomplete, then a popular version of Aestheticism became relevant for a mass of the population.

Alexander Keighley, an 'impressionist in photography', was described as 'an amateur who, unrestrained by the imperious demands of patrons, is free to use his photography for the satisfaction of his own aesthetic sense, and desiring no recognition or applause for the display of dexterity or skill, he seeks the sympathy of those to whom Nature appeals . . .'

'It is interesting to note that the photography of today, which is thus so largely due to genuine amateur effort, may be said to exist in direct proportion as the love of Nature out of doors characterises the English people.

'Although assuming greater dignity than a mere hobby or occasional pastime, photography only occupies Mr Keighley in his leisure from more imperious duties, yet the relationship between the man and his work is interesting to note; for Mr Keighley is before anything else a Naturalist. . . . His writings, his pictures, his conversation, show that the great hills, the scattered boulders, the trees and meadows . . . impress him only as an organic whole, yet as often as may be introducing by subtle suggestion a tender human interest . . .'[37]

These remarks by Horsley Hinton were a particularly full expression of the tangled enthusiasm for Nature and for the unique talent. In true amateur fashion this was not explained in terms of recognised aesthetic values, but remained a mixture of many views. Since theoretical sources were undiscriminated, the claim for originality was enhanced amongst photographers. Nevertheless artistic sources were recognised, and because one consequential arbiter of contemporary taste was Whistler, it was possible for the photographers to strike a critical attitude and achieve a style that differentiated their work frm the conventional Fine Arts.

The Whistler 'Memorial Exhibition' of 1905 was reviewed in the *Amateur Photographer* by J. C. Warburg in the language of a popular version of art for art's sake. This movement had in effect dismissed ratiocination and along with it, quite incidentally, the didactic and anecdotal art still popular at the Royal Academy. The photographers were late in appreciating the earlier movements, and their sense of propriety would not have allowed the intrusion of Decadence. These facts served only to confirm them in the will to a contemporary 'photographic quality', or truth to means, because their work simply did not look like contemporary Art. The contemporary photographic style existed in the elevation of the mundane, and in the creation of an enclosed world empty of incident, and in 1905 Whistler seemed to suggest a worthy precedent.

'Whistler looked for beauty in the picture itself. A picture should be a picture, not a novel in disguise, nor a historic treatise, nor a disguised sermon, nor a catalogue of facts; that is one of the lessons which we may learn from the Whistler show'.[38]

Warburg praised the monochromatic and subdued colours in the oil paintings and continued,

'Thus, by the simplest means used with consummate mastery, is obtained a dignity never surpassed. There is no striving after effect, no orgy of colour, no shouting, no jarring note. Everything is in the right place, everything fits everything else in the picture, and fits the picture as a whole, and the whole is a master-piece'.[39]

This passage may be said to describe the basic photographic values of the times – apparent minimal effort, minimal means, limpid composure, and yet exact and taut composition, and overall composition to boot, in which no area of the image, even the blank areas, can be said to work against the total effect. Warburg could not forbear quoting the Sunday Times correspondent, who said that Whistler sought beauty and found truth.

The work of Warburg himself, Dudley Johnston, James Batkin, Charles Job and Malcolm Arbuthnot existed at a remove from the balanced compositions of Horsley Hinton. Generally, these men preferred the pigment processes, and used them almost to erase the subject matter. They rounded and smoothed the forms, and united them in shape and in tone. J. C. Warburg wrote:

'The barbarity of harsh contrasts, the garrulity of ineffectual detail, the crudity of awkward angles, or the weakness of sloppy curves, tolerated or even sought after at first, gradually became repugnant. We seek after subjects more harmonious and suave, strong but not crude, gentle without weakness, full but not crowded. We find that we can say more in fewer words, that we can get power without forcing effects, that an almost even tone may be more expressive than a multitude of details.'[40]

Fig.6 J. Dudley Johnston *Manchester - The River Medlock* 1906

It was acknowledged that each photographer would choose according to his temperament whether to accentuate the beauties of line or the modulations of tone, but the qualities of the processes entailed the eradication of detail and the emergence of form. J. C. Warburg described the style in conventional terms: it was the result of the search for 'expression, simplicity, breadth, and harmonious distribution of the masses'.[41] Warburg and Dudley Johnston insisted upon 'photographic quality', which in Johnston's words meant that the 'new art' should be allowed to 'evolve its own conventions from its own necessities.'[42] The conventions in subject and treatment were still strongly reminiscent of Whistler (fig. 6) who said that the artist preferred to 'distill the refined essence' whereas the common man would be 'gratified' only with detail.

'And when the evening mist clothes the riverside with poetry, as with a veil, and the poor buildings lose themselves in dim sky, and the tall chimneys become campanili, and the warehouses are palaces in the night, and the whole city hangs in the heavens, and the fairy-land is before us – then the wayfarer hastens home; the working man and the cultured one, the wise man and the one of pleasure, cease to understand, as they have ceased to see, and Nature, who, for once, has sung in tune, sings her exquisite song to the artist alone . . .'[43]

This passage is not only a presentiment of Johnston's 'River Medlock', but of Charles Job's more prosaically stated aims – 'Simplicity of composition, a luminous atmosphere, and a feeling of restfulness'. To give 'a real impression of the original picture as I saw it in nature'.[44]

The idea that the 'original picture' existed in nature as simple, restful, and luminous is a measure of the neoplatonic strain in current principles even though they were much affected by Aestheticism. Of course it was the refined condition of Aestheticism that enabled the photographers to satisfy the demands of beauty and truth, which were transcendant and general. The refinement also let them claim for themselves the creative imagination. When the imagination was a passive receptacle that just recognised the moment of art then the resultant photographs drew near Walter Pater's vision of the Grecian Frieze as an expression of the 'colourless, unclassified purity of life'.[45]

The photographers offered delicate equivalences for the world that were probably equal in their skein of principles to much contemporary Fine Art. Indeed in 1908 Sickert felt he had to warn against the enthusiasm for Whistler, whose art was dangerous not so much for its visual aspect as for the emotions of the audience which if encouraged would defeat the sense of high purpose in art.[46] In 1910 he wrote:

'The more our art is serious, the more will it tend to avoid the drawing room and stick to the kitchen. The plastic arts are gross arts, dealing joyously with gross material facts . . . and while they will flourish in the scullery, or on the dunghill, they fade at a breath from the drawing room'.[47]

Whistler belonged to the age of the dandy, and an exquisitely refined taste, which as far as Sickert was concerned was no longer a possible modern attitude. But it was a considerable force in contemporary life, and though taste might approve different forms, there were some forms that were definitely bad taste. The characteristics of good taste were never defined, although they were often described, unhelpfully, as connected with beauty and nature. Hence the audience was confined to a narrow response.

In 1910 the exhibition 'Manet and the Post-Impressionists' opened at the Grafton Gallery, and was widely reviewed, provoking a lively correspondence in the daily press. The reviewer for the British Journal of Photography wrote:
'On entering, we were confronted by a gentleman loudly proclaiming the whole show to be a fraud and a swindle, while shrieks of laughter came from every room . . . The work of Cézanne, Sanguin (sic) Van Sogh (sic), Matisse and a few others, is so outrageous that we can convey no idea of it. It raises many laughs, but is beneath criticism. It was quite refreshing to find that no single person in the rooms was foolish enough to mistake any of the pictures for art, and the universal laughter was a reminder that the much-despised British public is made up of very honest art critics, whose opinion very fortunately carries considerable weight.'[68]

Some established artists were quoted: Sir Philip Burne-Jones called the Post-Impressionists 'execrable draughtsmen': E. Wake Cook called the show a 'Morgue'; and Sir William Richmond 'best summed up the show as one of 'hysterical daubs' '.

The threat against tradition and propriety was countered by the hostility of the professional classes; presented with the ridiculous 'art' of the Post-Impressionists, the Academicians and the amateur photographers closed ranks. One part of the threat was directed at the common view of beauty and truth. Many pictorial photographers continued to believe in an essential condition for beauty and truth, and their work during the following years, whilst giving pleasure and satisfaction, no longer played any part in the continuing debate about art and photography.

Other photographers were prepared to open themselves to further puzzlement. In 1911 the painter William Rothenstein spoke to the members of the

London Salon of Photography, and 'left his hearers almost without words'. He had no knowledge of photographic exhibitions, but the Salon filled him with despondency. Everyone 'seemed to be imbued with the idea that vague sentiment was part of the world of art', whereas Michael Angelo and Raphael or any of the old masters had 'got their poetry through the perfect statement of fact'. He refuted the exquisite, the vague and the feeble, and proclaimed the age of trumpet blasts and military music. Rothenstein urged his audience to read Homer and the Icelandic sagas and 'observe the brutality of the adherence to primal facts. As to the poetry below those facts, could they not trust to the observer to assimilate it without any vague poetising of their own?' It seems that Rothenstein's speech was 'resented' and it was certainly ignored. The resentment sprang from what appeared to be the stress upon the excellence of record photography:

'We placed on the walls of our schools maps of the British Empire. How much might be done to set on record by means of photography the mighty and strident and wonderful things there were in the world'.[49]

Fig.7 A. L. Coburn *The Great Temple Grand Canyon* 1911-12

Such ideas were anathema to the art-photographer, who considered such 'facts' the 'artistic defects' of the commercial photographer. In Britain the photographer was expected to balance very finely the requisites of fact and fancy, or nature and the imagination.

In 1916 Alvin Coburn exhibited some photographs of 'Wild and boldly rendered scenery of Californian subjects', (fig. 7) in which his imagination was supposed to have got out of hand.[50] Coburn said that it was 'unkind' to call him a 'wild revolutionary person, impatient of conventional restraint'. He asserted that he loved nature and in making the Grand Canyon series in 1911-12 had suffered great physical hardship because of his desire to record his impressions. He suggested that the critic was in love with 'banal' nature, in a 'sentimental mood', perhaps 'a nice pastoral landscape with plenty of woolly sheep'.[51]

The monumental efforts of Coburn to establish in England another view of nature, and even to break with nature altogether for a while in order to assess the future of pictorial photography, are described in the following section. It is sufficient to remark that his efforts met with virtually no response from the British.

In 1916 the Vorticist portraits of Ezra Pound and M. de Zayas were shown at the London Salon, and alongside the vortographs J. C. Warburg exhibited 'The Olive Tree – an Essay in Vorticism'. There were many more pictorial photographs related to the war. The pictorialists, who had found the world brazen and wished only to deliver it golden, were in disarray after the war, if Vorticism was irrelevant, then the pictorialists' relation to the war effort was confined to heroics, since, in Mortimer's words 'Art swells the roll of volunteers'. The pictorialists continued to occupy the Salons, and practise the manipulative processes; indeed a new generation, men such as Harold Leighton and Colin Unsworth, were ready to continue the time-honoured practices. However the old debate – was photography one of the fine arts? – was quite dead since the conception of art as painting in gold frames was itself finished. Art now lay in trash, caprice, abstraction and neoclassical severity, and save in the Rayogram and similar experiments the photographer no longer followed in the wake of the avant-garde. Art and photography took up their self-appointed tasks. Art was full of the sub-conscious, or self-referential, deeply romantic and mostly unrelated to the world at all, whereas photography sought to latch onto the world through the elimination of light and the reintroduction of the great shibboleth of the Victorian age, fact.

21

Fig.8 Original vortograph ink drawing used on the cover of the exhibition pamphlet of A. L. Coburn's show at the Camera Club 1971 *Vortographs and Paintings*

Fig.9 A. L. Coburn *Vortograph* 1917

But the re-emergence of fact in photography was altered totally by 'imagism' and the relativist and surface aesthetic values of the new age. It has been said that pictorial photography became fossilised, which as a term of disapproval is dubious since it seems to accept the harsh judgment of the established modernists. We feel no compunction in accepting Paul Strand's dismissal of pictorial photography after the war even whilst we regard the same as an indication of his place in the avant-garde. The aesthetic baggage of the avant-garde is for us quite as cumbersome as a disjointed view of the picturesque must have been in 1920, and both have been advantageously shed.

The strength of the pictorialists lay in their sceptical approach to innovation, which was an attitude they had always maintained, and in the conservative and professional middle classes it is an attitude that is not surprising. Indeed it may be a source of redemption, since the work produced does have some of the quality of the period that we recognise elsewhere.

Photography in Britain 1900-1920 was deliberate, and concerned with the erasure of fact. The single fault was that the contribution of conformist art, in closing the tradition of art for art's sake, was based on theoretical values that were insufficiently energetic to meet the demands of modern life. Whilst acknowledging that the achievements of the avant-garde brought about the total isolation of photo-pictorialism, no achievement in a minor key could withstand from its own advocates the effect of mild approbation.

ALVIN LANGDON COBURN

From 1900-1920 the propaganda struggle between the American and British art photographers was continuous, but one point at least was commonly held: everyone agreed that there was something radically different about the work produced by the photographers of each nation.

'This difference is not a mere difference of method or mannerism, but an entire difference of principle. European photographers treat pictorial photography as though it were a new method of art expression and present their subject in a manner which is not dissimilar from that which they would have employed with brush and pencil. American photographers, on the other hand, treat pictorial photography as a new departure . . . to the American each photograph is an experiment. . . .'[52]

This difference that was supposed to exist between the British and American pictorialist is especially difficult to recover now, except to say for instance that Annie Brigman or George Seeley were unreservedly Symbolist in a way never approached by the British.

But if the British rejected Symbolism, at least in its magical aspects, they also disdained work that looked like a more modern distortion. 'Epilogue' (plate 39), by Edward Weston, was thought to be a failure by one conservative critic because it was totally unnaturalistic, and though it seems today to be a tentative confection of aesthetic and popular cubist styles, it does bear out the American claim to contemporaneity which ran like a refrain through the descriptions of the Salons.

The critical response to the work of Alvin Coburn was especially revealing. Coburn was accused of breaking the rules of pictorial composition in 'Spiders

Web – Liverpool' 1906 (plate 6). The critic said he,

'would like to cut off the heavy piece of opaque reflection at the bottom, which has too little at the top as its counterpart to have a full meaning, and only suggests the beginning of a new composition, rather than the completion of this one'.[53]

Frederick Evans was so disturbed by this breach of the rules that he declared Coburn deficient in knowledge of composition. Other critics were much more circumspect and were prepared to believe that Coburn was attempting something new. A. J. Anderson wrote,

'Is he not in danger of learning to see with a photographic eye? Take Coburn's 'Spiders Threads', for instance. I know that I have never seen water reflections as he has depicted them – black, clear-cut, fossilized, as though the mast and rigging were reflected from a surface of corrugated steel'.

The critic affected not to have enjoyed this experiment – there should have been the suggestion of movement in the water – but in the end he decided that;

'One must own that the strong, convincing photographs of Alvin Langdon Coburn plead in their frank photography for belief in the American theory of the science-art'.[54]

More flexible than anyone, Coburn traversed the aesthetic terrain between Whistler and Wyndham Lewis, between the modulation of the 'Thames at Wapping' into a tissue of sensible shades, and Vorticism, iconoclastic and disintegrative, to which Coburn contributed in 1917 the first abstract photographs, known as vortographs (fig. 9). The glory of these experiments has been somewhat dimmed, probably because we are too familiar with the bromide process and reject kaleidoscopic abstractions as mannerisms. Yet if one remembers the climate in which such images were made they cease to be unconsidered frivolities. Nonetheless in the history of photography Coburn's wide achievements have been overshadowed by this sally into modernism. Coburn's photographic work for the jounals covered theatre,[55] portraits of the famous in 'Makers of Movements'[56], photo-reportage,[57] photo-journalism[58] and war-time propaganda.[59] In his art-photography Coburn dealt with modern subject matter such as 'The Flip Flap at the Franco-British Exhibition' (fig. 10).[60] He illustrated books[61] as well as producing photographic editions of artists work (fig. 11). He was extremely interested in the colour work of Lumiere, and expected it to distinguish professional work from the amateur, as well as to widen the gaps that existed between certain kinds of professional practice. At a restaurant in London he explained his new enthusiasm.

'Look here. You see this omelette, this glass of cider, this farcically arranged bunch of polychromatic flowers? Ain't they turr'ble? Don't the colours fairly screech? Well, that's nature. But look here. I take this omelette and place it here; I take this one flower of bright clear gold and put it on the white tablecloth beside it; and I place this glass of cider close beside it again, but in a place where the sun can catch it and give the colour a little more life. And there you have a very beautiful scheme. Well, that's art; that's photography. And that's what your amateur will never be able to do . . . (The new colour photographer) must reject, and arrogantly reject, and then he must rely on the residue with an absolute faith-

Fig.10 A. L. Coburn *Flip Flap* 1908

Reproductions · of · Works by Frank Brangwyn ∅ ∅ ∅
1. Kew Bridge · ∅ ∅ ∅ ∅ ∅
2. The · Return · of · the Caravan · ∅ ∅ ∅ ∅ ∅ ∅ ∅ ∅
3. The Vegetable Market Venice · ∅ ∅ ∅ ∅ ∅ ∅ ∅ ∅ ∅
4. The Departure of Blake
5. Santa · Maria · Della Salute ∅ ∅ ∅ ∅ ∅ ∅ ∅ ∅ ∅
Photographed & Published by Alvin Langdon Coburn London & New York · ∅ ∅
· MCMV ·

Fig.11 A. L. Coburn *Reproduction of Works by Frank Brangwyn* 1905

23

Fig.12 A. L. Coburn *New York Stock Exchange* 1909

fulness and humility . . . And its precisely because of my Whistlerian fidelity to chosen essential Nature that this new process interests me so much.'[62]

Coburn put his enthusiasm for the autochrome to immediate practical use – he photographed the Whistler paintings in the Charles L. Freer collection, and these were used by Charles Caffin in a lecture on Whistler at the Detroit Museum of Art in 1909. Caffin said 'Whistler hated the obvious. . . . He realised that if we are bound upon facts, we will feel only facts. He understood, none better, the powers of suggestion'. The transfiguration of Whistler's nocturnes by the auto-chromes was such that each picture thrown upon the screen 'excited spontaneous bursts of applause' for its 'luminosity'[63] Coburn opposed himself to Demachy (a gummist juggler) and Horsley Hinton (a crazy quilter) because he tried to see the little piece that matters in the midst of nature's messiness, and . . . concentrate the interest on that. That done, I use every inch of my knowledge to retain the purely photographic qualities', which did not mean the 'shrewish acidity' of pure lens work but 'photographic in the sense that Whistler was photographic . . . and that Leader isn't.'[64]

Coburn learned composition from Arthur W. Dow, the American landscape painter, who taught at Pratt Institute, Brooklyn and at the Art Students League, New York. Dow also held a summer school in Ipswich, Massachusetts and in 1903 Coburn contributed a group of photographs to the Summer School Exhibition.[65] Arthur Dow, who had been a curator of Japanese Art in the Museum of Boston (1897) wrote a book called 'Composition' (1899), in which he set out the importance of design as the aesthetic force of art.

'. . . a pictorial composition is not merely an assemblage of objects truthfully represented, it is the *expression of an idea*, and all the parts must be related as to form a harmonious *whole*. It cannot be a work of *art* unless it has this quality of wholeness . . . We feel the need of a new faculty which is but imperfectly de-developed; in short, the ability to *compose*, the *creative* faculty, not the imitative'.[66]

Coburn had a strong sense of design, but he was not confined to a British subject matter. The supposed existence of a picturesque Britain was one of the mainstays of British photographers, one of the reasons for their inability to embrace modernism within the confines of art-photography, and one source of dissatisfaction amongst American workers who complained 'we have not the picturesque landscape or the quaint costumes of some of the old countries . . . American light is so cruel that you can get any amount of plucky brilliant stuff but seldom anything soft and delicate'. The critics' response was to point to the picturesque sleighs, the variety of facial types, and the woods and creeks of Buzzard's Bay as strong enough in pictorial qualities to rival the 'mud-land marsh' school of Britain.

'Along the Susquehanna and its tributaries from near York, Pa., to Altoona, I have today seen hazy, soft effects as fine and dim outlines as picturesque as anything ever pictured by an exhibiting photographer, and I am told that these conditions have lasted for a fortnight.'[67]

Such atmospheric or impressionist photography was practiced among the Americans, notably by Rudolph Eickemeyer, but Coburn brought to Britain another, more dominant aspect of life in America, exemplified by the 'Stock Exchange, New York' (fig. 12).

'The glimpse into Wall Street is all American and local. Nowhere in Europe, nowhere outside America, will you see such a cliff of material achievement above a black froth of people. They do not break against it in waves; they just ripple along at the foot'.[68]

H. G. Wells compared the volume *New York* (1910) with the book of photographs of *London* (1909) and concluded that they 'quadruple their value if you look at them together'. He compared two photographs in particular, 'The Tunnel Builders' (plate 23) set in an excavation in New York, and 'Kingsway' (fig. 13) in which men work from a horse-drawn cart.

'In both volumes ... Mr Coburn has chanced to picture men at work. In the London picture the men form an amiable group, prevailing over a manifestly manageable job, but in the New York one ... it is the machine and enterprise that prevail'.[69]

Coburn himself felt that the photographer could make an artistic equivalence for the modern 'nature' of city life.

'As I steamed up New York harbour the other day on the liner that brought me home from abroad I felt the kinship of the mind that could produce those magnificent Martian-like monsters, the suspension bridges, with that of the photographer of the new school. The one uses his brain to fashion a thing of steel girders, a spider's web of beauty to glisten in the sun, the other blends chemistry and optics with personality in such a way as to produce a lasting impression of a beautiful fragment of nature'.[70]

Fig.13 A. L. Coburn *Kingsway* 1906

For some people 'Nature' was the countryside, or physiognomy, and less popularly the city, and it existed quite independently of themselves, pristine, but somewhat imperfect. The condition of Nature as material for the creative mind was familiar. H. P. Robinson had said,

'A work of art is a work of order, and if the artist is to put the stamp of his own mind on his work, he must arrange, modify, and dispose of his materials so that they may appear in a more agreeable and beautiful manner than they would have assumed without his interference.'[71]

These remarks were commonly accepted and though some would have demurred at Robinson's insistance that to gain the effect 'a house may be pulled down or a tree uprooted'[72] few would have balked at this kind of elimination, or addition, in the studio. The 'new school' of photography that Coburn was talking about regarded 'Nature' in another light: it was useless to alter the contingent world to suit a preordained and arbitrary set of compositional rules. The photographer accepted a more difficult task, and a more thoroughly modern conception of art was satisfied, if he looked into the arbitrary world for a pattern that perhaps made no sense at all in terms of the keys to compositional harmony. Order did not exist in any abstract grid that might be placed over the world and shifted about until the distribution of shapes was balanced; instead order existed in an imperfect state in the mind of the artist, and he found an objective correlative for his own idea of the world. This gained credence as art because it was composed, and retained its integrity as a photograph because it had a level of

Fig.14 A. L. Coburn *Station Roofs, Pittsburg* 1910

Fig.15 A. L. Coburn *The Death Glide* 1914

redundancy unacceptable in any other medium.

In 1906 Coburn held a one-man exhibition at The Royal Photographic Society and won some notice from the preface, written by G. B. Shaw, who claimed that Coburn's portraits were superior to those of Hals, Bellini, Gainsborough or Holbein. But as the reviewer said, 'after all, we cannot hold Mr Coburn responsible for Mr Bernard Shaw',[73] and the photographs themselves were well received. Part of this exhibition travelled to the rooms of the Liverpool Amateur Photographic Association in Eberle Street and occasioned one of the most significant critical essays of the period.
'Photography has been with us quite a number of days now, and it is really more than time that we relinquished our ingenuity, that we showed some comprehension of her qualifications, of her instincts, her unique abilities'[74]

The reviewer said that Coburn was not the artist who would declare the 'unprecedented genius' of photography, but he was at least 'an immediate precursor'. Coburn

'has seen that the real Photograph, the Photograph of the Future, is neither the clear, sharp, fiercely accurate record beloved by the honest gentlemen of the old anti-sentimental school nor the 'pictorial' affair, the affair that reminds you of a Whistler or a Constable, or a Corot, evolved by the aid of all manner of cabalistic and, (in the eyes of the purists) more or less questionable devices, by the later 'artistic' school. Mr Coburn has had the coolness (need I say that he is an American?) to detach himself from the dusty quarrel of these two hostile factions; and standing a little apart in his delightfully discreet way, he has been shrewd enough to discern the futility of their arguments ... Mr Coburn has recognised, partially and instinctively, that the achievements of the Photographer must differ, in subject and intention, as profoundly as they already do in technique, from the achievements of the workers with brush and pencil ... The native concern of the camera must be with passages of contemporary actuality which are, in the first place, too full of vital complexities ever to be rightly recalled by the memory, or reconstructed by the imagination ...'

The author describes 'A City Scene': ...
tumult of traffic, a fluent interweaving of cabs; carriages, lorries, electric cars, tentatory policemen, sporadic pedestrians – lamp-posts uplift here and there a crystalline poignancy, there is an acute entanglement of over-head wires, massed buildings, patterned with swift incidents of light and shade, stand in monotoned cliffs on this hand and on that ... Well, that, in spite of its multiplex detail, in spite of the ceaseless unstability of its incidents, presents an effect fairly stable and protracted. Its atoms spin, and lurch, and disappear, but the general attitude of the thing is fairly constant. A painter could render it: painters have rendered it. But in another instant something happens which thrusts the painter utterly out of court, and provides the Photographer with a motive that no art but his own has any power to utilize. North John Street spits out a sudden motor car. Its driver, flurried by the vortex, jerks and blunders ... a dramatic nucleus snatches and compels the whole whirling assemblage. For a fraction of time the effect hangs thus, – intimate, unanimous, organic, – every item within vision contributing to the fierce momentary tension. And then the strain slackens, the equability returns, the unique conspiracy of subtle notes vanishes irrevocably, and the Photographer's opportunity has come and gone'.[75]

The proto-futurist vortex and the obsession with the instantaneous may be seen in Coburn's 'Station Roofs, Pittsburgh', 1910 (fig. 14) and in 'The Death Glide', 1914 (fig. 15)[76] which was exhibited that year at The Royal Photographic Society. The reviewer would have found it difficult in 1906 to descant in this manner upon the work of British pictorialists. Coburn was not the Photographer of the Future, and never became it in the manner envisaged. Yet his efforts to make pictorial photography modern ensured his own removal from the centre to the edge of the establishment.

In 1913 a reviewer of Coburn's *Men of Mark* conceded that the personality of the photographer was apparently artless, but suggested that he was in fact an 'immensely cunning artist'.

'To the layman there seem broadly to be two sorts of photographs: Coburn's and other kinds ... (Coburn is) a man who expresses himself most easily in photography's three-ply alphabet of natural objects, novel patterns and new tones ... his opinions and impressions, not of the sensuous world only, spontaneously find their perfect equivalents among the shifting combinations of his craft.'[77]

Fig.16 A. L. Coburn *Gertrude Stein* 1913

In the spring of the same year Coburn went to Paris and he met Gertrude Stein. This portrait (fig. 16) is reminiscent of Picasso's painting of the writer (fig. 17) of 1906 which was published in *Camera Work* in a special number in June 1913. Coburn's portrait is inevitably more concerned than Picasso's with the pretensions of the sitter. No doubt Coburn was familiar with Stein's idiosyncratic prose style – her description of Picasso was printed in a special number of *Camera Work* in August 1912. A description of this style has been given by Wyndham Lewis, the vorticist whose attempts in England to establish an avant-garde helped dislodge Coburn as an establishment figure. According to Lewis the mannerism of Miss Stein in her writing is such that speech exists at a 'gibbering and baboonish stage'. Stein's bag of tricks allows her to force people into the category of 'those to whom things are done' – they speak in an 'infantile, dull witted, dreamy stutter', and they cease to speak in the manner of people who do things.[78] In Coburn's portrait Miss Stein appears at one moment to have become one of those to whom things happen, then she appears as the brilliant Jewish lady 'full of mystery and capable of subtle movements.'[79]

Fig.17 Picasso *Gertrude Stein* 1906

Coburn's contribution to the avant-garde movement in the arts demonstrated the isolated position of his colleagues in British photography. Coburn had taken a photograph of Wyndham Lewis, looking aggressive, seated in front of an abstract composition (fig. 18) and he wrote:

'Now, you know, I am very fond of these revolutionaries. They care not for the musty conventions of a classical art, or the vested interests of the art dealer. Theirs not to reason why, theirs but to square the cube and vorticise, as the spirit moves them'.'[80]

Fig.18 A. L. Coburn *Wyndham Lewis*

In 1916 Coburn's article entitled 'The Future of Pictorial Photography'[81] was published in the conservative annual *Photograms of the Year* which was edited by F. J. Mortimer (1912-1944). The article bears the traces of Coburn's association with the rhetoric of avant-gardism that was to be found in the Vorticist manifesto *Blast* (1914). Mortimer's sanguine acceptance of the squibs of slogan art should be seen in the context of a practice that was deeply embedded. It is easy with hindsight to see the decline of the pigment processes and the

Fig.19 A. L. Coburn *Vortograph No. 8* 1917

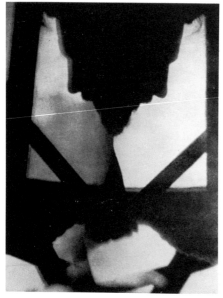

Fig.20 A. L. Coburn *Ezra Pound* 1916

extensive control that accompanied them. It must be said that for contemporaries, the continuous refinements of the bromoil process alone must have secured for it a place in pictorial photography that would not quickly be superseded.

The article pointed nicely to the uncertainties that faced the pigmenters concerning their relationship with those new art forms of Europe that offered a fresh conception of what it meant to be 'true to Nature'. In 1917 one of Coburn's Vortographs was reproduced in *Photograms* (fig. 19). A reviewer of the show said that experiment had led Coburn into a 'wild region . . . Something strange was bound to happen when the sane guidance of Nature was rejected'.[82] But Coburn had scored a palpable hit against the settled establishment. It is typical of him that his article should display an aspect of the fashionable, and typical also, for his reputation was deserved, that he should have been so acute in his diagnosis of the failings of contemporary pictorial photography.

In his article Coburn called for experimentation – he championed exactly the use of prisms to split images into segments which provided his vortograms of Ezra Pound (fig. 20). He had also photographed the writer using multiple exposures – another of the neglected possibilities of the camera with which he had but 'slightly experimented' and which he clearly felt offered a path away from the 'hollow and dull' work of recent years which was a state of affairs obvious to everyone no matter how suspicious they were of 'the modern movement in the arts.'

He wanted to 'throw off the shackles of conventional representation', but he was hard put to suggest any stirring means towards this end. He suggested that shutter speeds be developed to study movement, that successive exposures of an object in motion should be repeated on the same plate; the study of 'neglected' or 'unobserved' perspectives; designs visible under the microscope should be put to pictorial use; the use of prisms and time-lapse photography. None of these devices was impracticable, though it is true that they were not much used because they were irrelevant to the demands of exhibition work.

Then he struck the note of exasperation;

'Do something outrageously bad if you like, but let it be freshly seen . . . If it is not possible to be 'modern' with the newest of all the arts, then we had better simply bury our black boxes'.

What appears to have annoyed Coburn so much was that men were content to 'go on fishing out old negatives and making a few feeble prints of them', just as we have been doing for the past ten years, and if this continued 'photography will stagnate'. This is no more than a description of a common practice and the promise of stagnation that was supposed to result from this must have seemed nonsensical. There are numerous examples of F. J. Mortimer, for one, using old negatives to illustrate articles in the *Amateur Photographer* and for exhibition purposes, before, during and after the war. Coburn fired his salvo from a publication that represented the very people he wished to hit – the establishment figures who redressed old negatives – often small portions of old negatives to boot – and his salvo caused no radical or even minimal realignment,

Coburn tried to explain himself to the Camera Club. He

'had often asked himself why photography should not take part in modern art movements. Therefore, he went to Mr Ezra Pound, 'The high priest of Vorticism', and after a long talk they parted with drawings of the first vortoscope, and the name of the new art had been invented. Mr Pound, continuing the discussion, said that the pleasure derived from a vortograph was simply the pleasure of pattern'.[83]

Ezra Pound had adopted an aggressive posture – 'proceeding on the assumption that, in any presentation of abstract art today, the majority of an audience was hostile'.[84] The audience response may have been well represented by the remarks of W. L. F. Wastell who said that rather than any vortograph he preferred 'Jack Frost' on the window pane, presumably because these abstractions were natural. The audience seem to have been baffled by Coburn, and perhaps resented the condescension of Pound. After all, had they not suffered in the past at the hands of artists, whose enthusiasm for novelty or distortion remained incomprehensible. And at last Coburn had turned from his Whistlerian style and subsequent experiments, towards the disintegrative qualities of light. But unlike Edward Weston he did not turn to the 'sharply focussed . . . thing itself' which later became photographic modernism. The version of modernism that Coburn almost reached was the removal of the camera altogether. Light became the thing itself in the abstractions of Man Ray, Christian Schad, Moholy-Nagy and Bruguiere.

As the perceptive reviewer of 1906 had guessed, Coburn was not the Photographer of the Future. Yet he contributed more than any other to the gradual understanding of some aspects of American life. This may be seen in a review of 1916, in which the critic, buried in the notion that art deals with eternal truths, nonetheless appreciated the peculiar American contribution.

'In earlier years, and may be even today, we perhaps failed to appreciate and understand the outlook of American photographs. To some of us it appeared, at the first shock, to indicate a revolutionary movement involving the deposition of the gentle and the beautiful, and the enthronement of the brutal and the trivial . . . For dreaming landscape the American had apparently no further use; the decorative quality of his pictures seemed based on a geometrical design, woven out of sky-scrapers, high level railways, electric standards, and chaotic arteries of commerce . . . And yet it should be fairly easy for us to thread our way through the labyrinth to 'The American point of view' . . . His marvellous environment of mechanical, engineering and architectural achievement flatters his national pride . . . It has given him a new objective world, and added a new view of psychology to his literature . . . Emerson talks somewhere about 'the immobility of art – its absence of elasticity' a description which we have no difficulty in accepting if it be compared with the preoccupations of active life, for art, in its higher forms, is essentially contemplative, and occupies itself with the eternal, rather than the temporal, aspect of things.

To the American temperament this immobility would naturally be more perceptible and irksome than to us, and it may be that the American photographic trifle is the futile protest against a natural truth, of a people possessed of more sensitiveness but less artistic restraint than the older races. Whatever may be the true explanation of this phenomenon, we may depend upon it that the American has still further surprises in store for us. His wit and resource are inexhaustible and irrepressible. Indeed a vorticist portrait by one of them already bows, or rather jerks, you out of the door of this year's Salon'.[85]

Many of these remarks are a compendium of the beliefs that ensured the eclipse of British pictorialists after the First World War. To hear an Edwardian speak of the 'artistic restraint of the older races' need not be discomfiting. It is too easy to dismiss such views as prejudice without regard to the imperturbable conventions that are revealed. Faced with traditional responses within the arts and wider traditions in society, the artist found it difficult to obey the imperative of individuality. The work of Alvin Langdon Coburn is a signal example of the complexity of artistic response within the bounds of accepted art, and the artistic complexity of entertaining new formulae. The work of Coburn, and the public attitudes that greeted the work, demonstrated that the clash and synthesis of tradition and talent might never be fully realised. The individual talent nurtured upon traditional values, was forced to disengage itself, and dismiss nature as the source of art. The result was some notoriety and much misunderstanding, as well as real isolation, but within a few years the vortographs had become part of the tradition of the avant-garde. Today it is the earlier photographs that command attention since their success lay in discrete differences from the conventional patterns: such discontinuities show the real strength of the pictorial tradition.

John Taylor
1978

FOOTNOTES

[1] Albert Boime, *The Academy and French Painting in The Nineteenth Century*, London (1971).
[2] Emile Zola, 'III Present Day Art', *Mon Salon*, (1866). Translation from E. G. Holt, *From the Classicists to the Impressionists: A Documentary History of Art and Architecture*, New York, (1966), p. 380.
[3] 'The Photographic Salon des Refusés', *The British Journal of Photography*, (2 October 1908) p. 753
[4] W. A. Stewart, 'To the Editors, The Salon Selection Committee', *The British Journal of Photography*, (25 September 1908) p. 745.
Steichen showed thirty nine works, and Coburn showed twenty one. The five Americans on the committee were Coburn, Eugene, Steichen, Stieglitz and White. Of these Steichen and Coburn performed the 'actual work of selection in London'. Joseph Keiley of New York was reputed to have taken part in the selection, though his name did not appear in the Salon catalogue. The British selectors were Craig Annan, Arbuthnot, Benington and Davison.
[5] Frank Roy Fraprie, 'The English Photographic Exhibitions', *American Photography*, (November 1908), p. 620.
[6] From January 1909 until May 1917 when exhibitions at '291' ceased, the only photographic exhibitions were one-man shows of the work of Coburn, de Meyer, Steichen, Stieglitz and Strand. There were no exhibitions of members' work. For the details see William Innes Homer, *Alfred Stieglitz and the American Avant-Garde*, London (1977) pp 296-8.
[7] 'The Photographic Salon des Refusés', *The British Journal of Photography*, (2 October 1908), p. 753.
[8] The Selection Committee consisted of J. Craig Annan; Malcolm Arbuthnot, Walter Benington; George Davison; (these four had served on the discredited 1908 Selection Committee); Reginald Craigie; Frederick H. Evans; J. Dudley Johnston; F. J. Mortimer.
[9] 'The Ways of Selecting Committees – Salon and Royal', *The British Journal of Photography* (18 September 1908), p. 721.
[10] 'The American Photo-Secession', *The Photographic News*, (3 January 1908), p. 16.
[11] H. Snowden Ward 'The London Salon of Photography', *American Photography*, (December 1910), p. 692.
[12] Letter from G. Davison to M. Arbuthnot, 20 June 1910. A copy of this letter was sent to A. Coburn by Davison on the same day. George Eastman House 75:058:190.
[13] The members of 'The London Secession' were Annan, Arbuthnot, Benington, Calland, Coburn, Archibald Cochrane, Davison, J. Dudley Johnston, Baron de Meyer, Frank H. Read. The invited

exhibitors were the Photo-Secessionists Annie Brigman, Frank Eugene, Mrs Kasebier, Heinrich Kuehn, Edward Steichen, Alfred Steiglitz and Clarence White.
See 'The London Secession Camera Pictures Exhibition', *Photography and Focus*, (16 May 1911), p. 409.

14 Ibid. F. J. Mortimer, editor of *The Photographic News* (1906-1908), was elected a Link in 1907.

15 F. J. Mortimer, 'The London Secession', *The Amateur Photographer* (15 May 1911), p. 476.

16 A. J. A. (A. J. Anderson). 'A Note on Two Pictures by Mrs Annie Brigman in this Issue', *The Amateur Photographer*, (8 March 1910), p. 236.

17 Alfred Stieglitz, *Photo-Secessionism and its Opponents: Five Recent Letters*, New York, (August 1910), p. 16.

18 F. J. Mortimer's editorial 'The Self-Seeker', *The Amateur Photographer*, (20 September 1910), p. 276.

19 Alfred Stieglitz, *Photo-Secessionism and its Opponents, Another Letter – The Sixth*, New York, (20 October 1910), p. 8.

20 See 21 below; also H. Snowden Ward, 'An American Complaint', *American Photography*, (March 1909), p. 135.

21 H. Snowden Ward, 'Suggestions to Would-be Picture-makers', *Photograms of the Year*, (1903), p. 51.

22 Gleeson White, 'The Great Exhibitions', *Photograms of the Year*, (1896), p. 67.

23 'Tendencies', *Photograms of the Year*, (1897), p. 8.

24 (H. Snowden Ward), 'The Divine Idea in Composition', *Photograms of the Year*, (1902), p. 40.

25 'Pictorial Photography from America', *The Amateur Photographer*, (12 October 1900), p. 282.

26 G. Bernard Shaw, 'The Exhibitions', *The Amateur Photographer*, (11 October 1901), p. 284.

27 H. Vivian Yeo, 'The American School and Mr Steichen's Pictures', *The Amateur Photographer*, (1 May 1902), p. 346.

28 Bernard Shaw, 'Some Criticisms of the Exhibitions', *The Amateur Photographer*, (16 October 1902), p. 307.

29 *Ibid.*

30 A. Horsley Hinton, 'A Note on the Construction of a Picture', *The Amateur Photographer*, (9 October 1902), p. 285.

31 Frederick H. Evans, 'Camera-Work in Cathedral Architecture', *Camera Work*, No 4, (1903), p. 18.

32 A. J. Anderson, 'A Last Word on Vagueness', *The Amateur Photographer*, (3 March 1904), p. 169.

33 J. A. M. Whistler, *The Red Rag, The Gentle Art of Making Enemies*, reprint of 1892 edition, New York, (1967) p. 126.

34 Will A. Cadby, 'Whistler, and the Gentle Art of – Photography', *The Amateur Photographer*, (2 June 1904), p. 436.

35 J. A. M. Whistler 'Propositions – No. 2', op. cit., p. 115.

36 Walter Pater, *Studies in the History of the Renaissance*, London, (1873), p. 213.

37 A. Horsley Hinton, 'Artistic Photography of Today', *The Amateur Photographer*, (11 October 1904), p. 288.

38 J. C. Warburg 'Watts and Whistler Part II', *The Amateur Photographer*, (11 April 1905), p. 301

39 *Ibid*.

40 J. C. Warburg, 'Pot-Hooks: An Apologia', *The Amateur Photographer*, (29 March 1910), p. 322. Reprint of 1892 edition, New York, (1967) p. 144.

41 J. C. Warburg, 'My Best Picture', *The Photographic News*, (3 May 1907), p. 356.

42 'The Future of Pictorial Photography in Great Britain – a symposium by the leading British Workers', *The Amateur Photographer*, (14 December 1909), p. 575.

43 J. A. M. Whistler, 'Ten O'Clock' (1885), op. cit., p. 144.

44 Charles Job, 'My Best Picture', *The Photographic News*, (22 March 1907), p. 232.

45 Walter Pater, op. cit., p. 191.

46 W. Sickert, The New 'Life of Whistler', *The Fortnightly Review*, December 1908, pp. 117-128.

47 W. Sickert 'Idealism', *Art News*, 12 May 1910.

48 The 'Post-Impressionists' at the Grafton Galleries, *The British Journal of Photography*, (2 September 1910), p. 911.

49 'Mr William Rothenstein at the London Salon', *The Amateur Photographer*, (2 October 1911), p. 324.

50 Anthony Guest, 'A One-Man show of pictures by Alvin Langdon Coburn, at Hampshire House', *The Amateur Photographer*, (13 March 1916), p. 204.

51 A. L. Coburn, 'Mr Coburn and Nature', a letter, *The Amateur Photographer*, (27 March 1916), p. 261.

[52] A. J. Anderson, 'The American Photographs at New Bond Street', *The Amateur Photographer*, (12 February 1907), p. 138.

[53] Frederick H. Evans, 'The London Photographic Salon for 1906', *Camera Work*, No. 17, (1907), p. 32.

[54] A. J. Anderson, op. cit., p. 138.

[55] For instance, A. L. Coburn illustration: 'A Ballad of Reading Gaol' of the Stage: 'Justice' by Galsworthy', *The Sketch* (9 March 1910), p. 279.

[56] A. L. Coburn, Portrait of Galsworthy, 'Makers of Movements' *The Bystander*, (31 December 1913).

[57] A. L. Coburn, 'Seven Illustrations for "The City of Mr Chamberlain". Birmingham and its new University', *The Pall Mall Magazine* (July 1909), p. 3.

[58] A. L. Coburn, 'The Last Phase: Windsor's Half Masted Flag.' (The Funeral of King Edward VII), *The Sketch*, (25 May 1910), p. 22.

[59] A. L. Coburn, 'The Eyes of the Army, Precision, Exactitude and Regularity: The Army's Perfect "Eyes",' *Illustrated London News*, (19 September 1914), p. 417.

[60] 'Art and Engineering – a Study at the Photographic Salon', *The Sphere*, (26 September 1908), p. 275.

[61] See *Alvin Langdon Coburn, an Autobiography* edited by Helmut and Alison Gernsheim, London, (1966), p. 141.

[62] The London Correspondent, 'The Painters New Rival – Colour Photography – an Interview with Alvin Langdon Coburn', *The Liverpool Courier*, (31 October 1907); reprinted in *American Photography*, (January 1908), p. 13.

[63] 'Value of Color Photographs Seen', *Detroit Free Press*, (24 April 1909). Coburn's Autochrome plates of Whistler's work are in the Permanent Collection of The Royal Photographic Society.

[64] *The Liverpool Courier* op. cit.

[65] 'Dow Exhibition at Ipswich', *Sunday Herald*, Boston, (9 August 1903).

[66] From Arthur Dow's address to Boston Art Students' Association 1894, quoted by Arthur Warren Johnson, *Arthur Wesley Dow*, Ipswich Historical Society, 1934 p. 61.

[67] H. Snowden Ward, 'An American Complaint', *American Photography*, (March 1909), p. 135.

[68] H. G. Wells, Foreword to *New York* by A. L. Coburn, London (1910).

[69] *Ibid*.

[70] A. L. Coburn, 'Artists of the Lens – The International Exhibition of Pictorial Photography in Buffalo', *Harpers Weekly*, (26 November 1910), p. 11.

[71] H. P. Robinson, *Picture Making by Photography*, reprint of 5th edition of 1897, Arno Press, New York, 1973, p. 44.

[72] *Ibid*, p. 45.

[73] O.M.H., 'Art from the Camera: Mr Bernard Shaw on Mr Langdon Coburn's Work', *Daily Chronicle*, (12 February 1906).

[74] D.S., 'The Function of the Camera, an Essay in Definition', *Liverpool Courier*, (16 May 1906). Part of this review was published in *The Amateur Photographer*, (29 May 1906), pp. 447-8.

[75] *Ibid*.

[76] A. L. Coburn ' "The Death Glide": a dive in the Clouds: a remarkable Photograph', *The Sketch* (16 September 1914), p. 289.

[77] D.S. (Dixon Scott), 'Magnificent Markmanship', *The Bookman*, (October 1913), p. 44.

[78] Wyndham Lewis 'Ernest Hemingway (The 'Dumb-Ox'), *Men Without Art*, London, 1934, p. 27.

[79] Gertrude Stein's *Three Lives* quoted in Wyndham Lewis ibid. p. 26.

[80] A. L. Coburn, *More Men of Mark*, London, 1922, p. 19.

[81] Reprinted in *Photographers on Photography*, edited Nathan Lyons, George Eastman House, (1966), pp. 53-55.

[82] Anthony Guest, 'Mr Coburn's Vortographs', *Photo Era* (May 1917), p. 227.

[83] 'Vorticism by Camera: pioneer Work in Vortography: Vortographed: 'The High Priest of Vorticism",' *The Sketch Supplement*, (14 March 1917), pp. 6-7.

[84] 'Mr Bernard Shaw on 'Vortography', The 'Coburns' at the Camera Club', *The Amateur Photographer* (19 February 1917), p. 116.

[85] J. W. Lumb, 'The Salon – A Retrospective Appreciation', *The Amateur Photographer*, (16 October 1916), p. 308.

THE PLATES

1

Walter Benington *Among the Housetops* 1900

2

A. L. Coburn *Wapping* 1908

3

J. Dudley Johnston *Liverpool – An Impression* 1907

4

Malcolm Arbuthnot *By the Sea* 1910

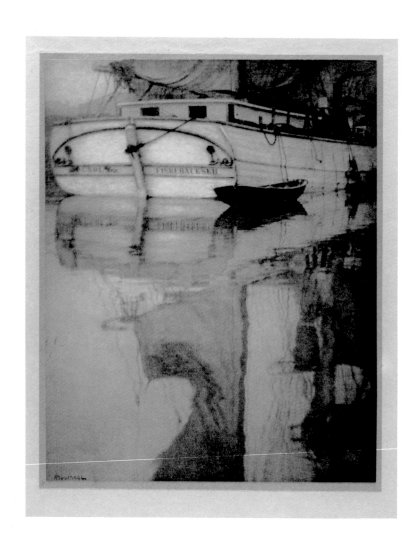

5

Malcolm Arbuthnot *Reflections* 1909

6

A. L. Coburn 'Spider's Web' – Liverpool 1906

7
Robert Demachy *L'Effort* 1904

8

John H. Anderson *Trawlers* 1913

9

Malcolm Arbuthnot *To Larboard* c.1907

10

John H. Anderson *The White Sail* c.1920

11
George Davison *The Long Arm* 1900

12
Theodor Hofmeister *The Solitary Horseman* 1900

The Pool   By Edward A. Steichen

13

Edward Steichen *The Pool* 1898

Fleeting and Far

14

A. Horsley Hinton *Fleeting and Far* 1903

15

J. Dudley Johnston *Corfe Castle* 1910

16

J. C. Warburg *Rushy Shore, Seaton* 1907

17

Charles Job *Morning Mist on the Sussex Downs* 1905

18
Alexander Keighley *Fantasy* 1915

19

J. Craig Annan *Bullock Cart, Burgos* 1913

20
Frank Eugene *The Horse* c.1908

21

J. C. Batkin *Whilst the Daylight lasts* 1908

22

E. Warner *Navvies* 1908

23

A. L. Coburn *New York, The Tunnel-Builders* 1908

24

Alfred Stieglitz *Going to the Post* 1904

25

Walter Benington *After the Storm* 1903

26

Paul Strand *Telegraph Poles* 1916

27

Frederick H. Evans *F. Holland Day in Algerian Costume* c.1901

28

Heinrich Kuehn *Untitled* (*Woman in Riding Habit*)

29
Rudolph and Mina Duhrkoop *Clotilde von Derp* 1913

30

J. B. B. Wellington *Mother's Jewels* 1917

31

J. O. Echague *Moro al Viento* 1909

32
Frank Eugene *Rebecca* 1901

33

E. O. Hoppé *Portrait of A. P. Allinson* c.1909

34

J. Craig Annan *The White House* 1905

35

Gertrude Kasebier *Untitled* (*Clarence White's son leaning on a Wall*)

36

Clarence White *The Cave* 1901

37

Baron A. de Meyer *Olga de Meyer* c.1900

38

Baron A. de Meyer *Portrait of a Man*

39
Edward Weston *Epilogue* 1919

40

Baron A. de Meyer *Hydrangea* c.1908

CHRONOLOGY

1878 Platinum paper sold commercially
1883 Photogravure process introduced to Britain
1883 Hamburg Exhibition of Pictorial Photography
Photo-Club (Paris) founded
Photographic Salon, 1st exhibition organised by the Linked Ring
1884 *Amateur Photographer* magazine founded
1885 Camera Club (London) established
c.1890 Das Kleeblatt founded
1891 Vienna Camera Club founded
1892 The Linked Ring Brotherhood founded from the secession of a
number of eminent pictorialists from the RPS
1894 Gum bichromate process developed for pictorial use
1895 *Photograms of the Year* founded
Gum bichromate process perfected
1896 New York Camera Club and Amateur Photographer merged to form
the Camera Club
1897 *Camera Notes*, journal of the Camera Club (ed. Stieglitz)

1900 *The New School of American Photography* 400 print exhibition organised by Day, Steichen and Coburn at the RPS Galleries
BPS (Birmingham) 1st Salon
1901 *The New School of American Photography* shown at the Photo-Club
of Paris
Glasgow International exhibition organised by Annan
Photography as a Fine Art by Charles Caffin published
1902 Stieglitz founds the Photo-Secession
1903 *Camera Work* founded, Evans is first English photographer to be
included
International Society of Pictorial Photographers founded, first
President J. Craig Annan
Autochrome process invented
1904 The 1st *Northern Exhibition* held in Liverpool, subsequently in turn
at Leeds (1905), Manchester (1906) and Liverpool (1907) etc.
Oil printing developed
1905 Little Galleries of the Photo-Secession opened at 291 Fifth Avenue.
Annan and Evans exhibited
1st commercial panchromatic plates
1907 *Modern Photography* exhibition at the New English Art Club, organised by Coburn and De Meyer, showing the work of 'seven shooting
starts' (Annan, Coburn, Day, Demachy, Kasebier, de Meyer, Puyo)
The Little Galleries of the *Amateur Photographer* become a 'recognised centre for the manifestation of progress in artistic photography'
Autochrome plates manufactured commercially
1908 De Meyer and Coburn exhibition at Goupil Gallery
American dominated Selection Committee of Photographic Salon
rejects work of eminent British pictorialists
Salon des Refusés organised by Mortimer at the *Amateur Photographer*
Little Galleries.
1909 Final exhibition and dissolution of the Linked Ring (membership
had included Annan, Anderson, Arbuthnot, Coburn, Benington,
Davison, Day, Demachy, Eickemeyer, Eugene, Evans, Hinton, the
Hofmeisters, Job, Johnston, Kuehn, Kasebier, Keighley, de Meyer,
Mortimer, Muir, Stieglitz, Steichen, Wellington, White)
1910 London Salon of Photography established
International Exhibition of Photography at the Albright Gallery,
Buffalo, organised by Stieglitz
Linked Ring collapses
Salon continues as London Salon Club
Hoppé exhibition at RPS
Roger Fry's Post-Impressionist exhibition in London
1911 Single exhibition of the London Secession at the Newman Gallery
(incl. Annan, Coburn, Benington, de Meyer, Stieglitz)

1912 *Photograms of the Year* edited by Mortimer
Arbuthnot takes Fry's Post-Impressionist show to Liverpool
1914 *American Invitation Collection* at RPS Exhibition (incl. Coburn, Day,
Eugene, Kasebier, Seeley, Stieglitz, Struss, White)
1915 Pictorial Photographers of America founded by Coburn, Kasebier,
Struss and White
1917 Final issue of *Camera Work*
'291' closed
Coburn's Vortographs
1920 London Salon of Photography continues to hold exhibitions (mem-
bership had included Anderson, Demachy, Duhrkoop, Eickemeyer,
Erfurth, the Hofmeisters, Job, Kasebier, Kay, Keighley, Misonne,
Mortimer, Muir, Wellington)
The RPS Annual Exhibition continues (membership had included
Batkin, Benington, Coburn, Demachy, Dell, Duhrkoop, Echague,
Evans, Hoppé, Job, Johnston, Keighley, Mortimer, Stieglitz, A. & J.
Warburg, Wellington)
1921 RPS Pictorial Group established

BIOGRAPHIES OF PHOTOGRAPHERS

JOHN H. ANDERSON

John Anderson lived in Barnes, London. Photographically, he was active between 1897 and 1937. He worked primarily in the gravure and platinum processes. During the late 1890's he began to exhibit at the Photographic Salon, and although his work was regularly selected, he was not elected to membership of the Linked Ring until 1906. In 1900 and 1901 a number of his prints were shown at the annual RPS Exhibition. After the dissolution of the Linked Ring, Anderson became associated with the London Salon of which he remained a member until 1937. Examples of his work were owned by Evans, Mortimer and Warburg.

J. CRAIG ANNAN 1864-1946

'One of the foremost artists in photography' Keiley, *Camera Work* 1904

James Craig Annan was born in Hamilton, Scotland, the son of the well-known photographer, Thomas Annan. In 1869 the family moved to Edinburgh where Thomas Annan used the studio of the early photographer and painter, D. O. Hill. The original calotype negatives made by Hill and Adamson were still stored at the studio. The move did not appear to be a success and within the year the Annans had returned to Glasgow.

Before leaving school, Craig Annan had acquired considerable knowledge of photographic processes and had come into contact with many artistic friends of his father, but his first interest was not in photography. In the early 1880's he studied chemistry and natural philosophy at Glasgow University.

In 1883 Craig Annan, interested by the recently perfected process of photogravure, accompanied his father to Vienna to study the technique under the inventor, Karl Klic. He brought his knowledge and expertise of the process back to Britain and to the family firm. In about 1890, Annan made a series of photogravures from the Hill and Adamson negatives, which brought this early work into prominence and later acclaim at the 1910 Albright exhibition.

In 1892 Craig Annan became interested in picture-making by photography He visited Holland with the artist, D. Y. Cameron; on their return they held a joint exhibition in Glasgow. The exhibition illustrated the 'possibilities of photography in comparison with older methods of transcribing nature'. This success encouraged a visit to Italy resulting in a Folio of gravures. Annan has claimed his work to be influenced by his friends of the Glasgow Impressionist School, Japanese prints, Velasquez and Whistler. Professionally Craig Annan continued his father's practice, mainly as a portrait photographer. He exhibited at the first Photographic Salon in 1893 and was elected to membership of the Linked Ring in 1895. During the next few years his prints were shown at the major exhibitions; in 1904 a selection of his gravures were published by Stieglitz in *Camera Work*; the same year he became the first President of the International Society of Pictorial Photographers.

Craig Annan continued to exhibit internationally until 1916, after which he concentrated on his professional work. He died at his home near Glasgow in 1946. The firm continues today as picture dealers with a small photographic studio.

MALCOLM ARBUTHNOT 1874-1967

'The most advanced of the moderns' Editorial, *Amateur Photographer* 1909

Malcolm Arbuthnot was born in London and spent his first years in East Anglia. After school he was apprenticed to the painter C. A. Brindley, in Suffolk, and later took up photography, becoming interested in the pigment processes.

In the early 1900's Arbuthnot perfected a commercially successful gum process and marketed the Lento-pigment paper. His work was first shown at the 1901 Photographic Salon of the Linked Ring, although he was not elected to membership until 1907, after a 'remarkable entry of 17 gum and oil prints' to the Salon. In 1909 he was a member of the Selection Committee for the last Photographic Salon. The following year he exhibited at the Vienna Exhibition and did not become involved with the new London Salon. He did exhibit again in London with a one-man show at the Little Gallery of the Amateur Photographer in 1910 and again at the Goupil Gallery in 1912.

Later in 1912 Arbuthnot was appointed Manager of Kodak's Liverpool branch and became associated with the Photographic Society in Liverpool. He continued to retain his earlier involvement with painting and in 1913 organised a Post-Impressionist exhibition at the Sandon Studios in Liverpool. In 1914 he was one of the original signatories to Wyndham Lewis's Vorticist Manifesto *Blast*. The same year he returned to London, where he continued to paint and also started a photographic portrait studio in New Bond Street. During the 1st World War his negatives were destroyed by fire, but he continued to run the studio until 1926.

Arbuthnot moved to Jersey in about 1930 and devoted himself to painting, studying under William Nicholson. He was elected a Fellow of the Royal Society of Arts in 1939 and a Member of the Royal Institute of Painters in Water Colours in 1944. He died in Jersey in 1967.

J. C. BATKIN 1867-1936

'The most successful exponent of multiple gum bichromate' Bernard Moore 1936

James Clarke Batkin was born in Aston, Birmingham, the son of Hannah (Clarke) and James Batkin. In 1887 he enlisted as a voluntary artilleryman with the Territorials, where he later became known as 'Snapshot Batkin'.

J. C. Batkin was a keen watercolourist and was able to apply his painting skills to the photographic printing process of gum bichromate. In 1898 he joined the Birmingham Photographic Society (BPS), then considered the most important society outside London. He became a member of the Hanging Committee in 1900 and for some time was the Chairman. He obtained his first medal at the 1903 BPS Exhibition, and the same year was elected to membership of the RPS where he began to exhibit. He was elected to the Council of the BPS in 1905. Batkin suffered from a speech defect and preferred not to take a prominent part in meetings, although he gave many successful demonstrations.

From 1914 Batkin gave up his photographic commitments under the pressures of Territorial and War work. He rejoined the BPS in 1919, but did not produce pictures for exhibition until 1935, when he obtained the only medal awarded to a BPS member.

Batkin died in 1936 in a London hospital from a disease contracted in Russia where he had been on holiday with his wife.

WALTER BENINGTON 1872- ?

'the finest pictorial impression of the heart of London' *Photographic Salon* review 1903

Walter Benington was born in Stockton in 1872. He worked in London as a block-maker, an occupation which led to acquaintance and friendship with many leading photographic workers of the day. He was an admirer and collector of Japanese prints.

Benington first exhibited at the Photographic Salon in 1900 and was elected to membership of the Linked Ring the following year. At the 1903 Salon his photograph 'The Church of England' was received with great acclaim and in 1904 he was awarded the Grand Prix at the St. Louis Exposition. He joined the RPS in 1907 and held a one-man show at their Galleries in 1908. As a member of the American dominated Selection Committee for the 1908 Photographic Salon, he was partly responsible for the rejection of the work of several notable pictorialists, which stimulated the formation of a Salon des Refusés and eventually led to the collapse of the Linked Ring. In 1910 his work was included in the single exhibition of the London Secession at the Newman Gallery. After 1910 he exhibited at the new London Salon and continued to show his work at the RPS, although he became disassociated from the organisation.

Throughout his involvement with the pictorial movement Benington worked from virtually untouched negatives. His prints were made primarily in platinum or gum. He wrote for the photographic press and during the early 1900's his work was frequently reproduced. During 1931 Benington moved to Oxford. He continued to exhibit his photographs at the London Salon until 1935.

ANNIE BRIGMAN 1869-1950

Ann Wardrope Nott was born in Honolulu, Hawaii, the eldest child of Samuel Nott from California. In 1886 the Notts returned to California, where Annie met and married sea captain Martin Brigman.

The earliest notice of Annie Brigman's work was at the San Francisco Photographic Salon (1903) which included work by the Photo-Secession. Many of Annie's early photographs portray her sister Elizabeth, whose work was also shown at the 1903 exhibition. Annie Brigman's work became widely exhibited both in America and in Britain, where she was regularly represented in London and Birmingham. In 1903 she was elected a member of the Photo-Secession and her prints were exhibited at '291'. In 1909 she exhibited at the National Art Club in New York and a selection of her photographs were published in *Camera Work*. She travelled to New York to see Stieglitz and '291', and stayed in New York for the following eight months. Brigman experienced some difficulties with technique; Stieglitz described the images as 'worthwhile, though often the way they were printed is rotten'. During 1910 Brigman separated from her husband and went to live with her mother in Oakland. Her work was shown at the Albright Exhibition (1910) and again in *Camera Work* in 1912.

After 1914 Annie Brigman photographed less, although she did show work at the 1st *Exhibition of Pictorial Photography* in San Francisco in 1922 and yearly continued to be represented in these exhibitions. During the 1930's she gave up photography, partly due to failing eyesight, and turned to writing poetry. In 1946 her first book of poems was published, it was illustrated by her early photographs (*Songs of the Pagan*).

Annie Brigman died in Oakland at the home of her sister Elizabeth in 1950, while still working on her second book.

A. L. COBURN 1882-1966

'The first purely abstract photographer' Vortographs 1917

Alvin Langdon Coburn was born in Boston, Massachusetts, the son of a prosperous shirt manufacturer. In 1889, after the early death of his father, Alvin and his mother moved to the Los Angeles home of his grandparents. The following year, at the age of eight, he was given his first camera. In 1891 he returned, with his mother, to Massachusetts.

In 1898 Coburn met a distant cousin, F. Holland Day, who further influenced him in photography. The next year Coburn and his mother were invited to accompany Day to London, where Day was planning to hold *The New School of American Photography* exhibition. The exhibition was held at the RPS Galleries, Coburn's work was accepted and at the RPS he met

Steichen and Evans. Several of Coburn's photographs were also shown at the Photographic Salon of the Linked Ring. In the new year Coburn accompanied Day to Paris where he met Eugene and Demachy. He returned to America in 1901 and in 1902 opened a studio on Fifth Avenue, not far from '291'. The same year he was elected a member of the Photo-Secession and in 1903 a member of the Linked Ring. His prints were reproduced in *Camera Work*; he held two one-man shows at '291', in 1907 and 1909.

In 1904 Coburn again visited England and began a lasting friendship with George Bernard Shaw, who provided contacts for many of the portraits published in *Men of Mark* (1913) and *More Men of Mark* (1932). In 1906 he began photographing for the illustrations of the work of Henry James, which were completed the next year. In 1906 he bought a house on the Thames at Hammersmith, learned the art of photogravure and started to produce his city books of *New York* and *London* (1910). In 1910 Coburn returned to America; he visited Buffalo, Pittsburg, the Yosemite Valley and the Grand Canyon. He married in America in 1912; in 1916 his wife accompanied him back to Britain, where they were invited to stay with George Davison at his North Wales home. The same year Coburn began his photographic records of the construction of Liverpool Cathedral and devised the Vortoscope, a triangular tunnel formed from three mirrors. The Vortographs were exhibited in 1917.

From 1919 Coburn became deeply involved with Freemasonry and photographed very little. In 1932, having lived in Britain for nearly twenty years, he decided to become a British subject and moved to Harlech, North Wales. The Coburns remained in North Wales, later moving to the warmer Colwyn Bay and spent many winters abroad, usually in Madeira, where Coburn again began to take photographs.

Coburn died at his Colwyn Bay home in 1966.

GEORGE DAVISON 1854-1930

'One of the pioneers of pictorial photography' Harold Baker 1931

George Davison was born in Lowestoft, the son of a ship's carpenter. His first employment was as an Audit Clerk at the Treasury.

Davison was an early practitioner of pictorial photography and, in 1885 he was one of the first members of the London Camera Club, of which he became Secretary the following year. The same year, 1886, he joined the RPS and in 1890 submitted the much acclaimed photograph *The Onion Field* (then entitled *An Old Farmstead*) to the annual Salon of the RPS, for which he gained a Society Medal. This image was believed, by his contemporaries, to mark the beginning of the Modern School of Pictorial Photography. The following year Davison, in a controversy over his late entries for the RPS Exhibition, was a major cause of the quarrels and misunderstanding, which in 1892 resulted in the secession of a number of eminent pictorialists from the RPS, the founding of the Linked Ring, and in 1893 the establishment of the Photographic Salon as a rival exhibition.

In 1897, Davison, who had become associated with the Kodak Company in 1889, was appointed Deputy Manager of the newly founded Kodak Limited in England. In 1900, following the sudden death of the Managing Director, Davison was appointed to succeed him, but in 1908 George Eastman considered him insufficiently committed and commercially suited to the position and asked him to resign, after which he was appointed to the Board of Directors. In 1907 Davison, who for some years had been associated with anarchist organisations, became more publicly involved, and was advised not to sit for re-election to the Board. He left Kodak a wealthy man and built a palatial mansion at Harlech, in Wales, where he continued his political activities, housed children from London slums and entertained extensively.

George Davison died in 1930 at his house in the South of France.

(We are indebted to Brian Coe for some of this information.)

F. HOLLAND DAY 1864-1933

Frederick Holland Day was born in Norwood, Massachusetts, the son of a wealthy leather merchant. Day was privately educated and able to travel extensively.

From 1884 he was employed in Boston by a firm of publishers, but in 1889 his increasing interest in Keats drew him to Europe in the company of his cousin, the poetess Louise Imogen Guiney. During his travels, Day took a number of photographs. On his return to Boston in 1891 he joined Herbert Copeland to form a publishing company. Copeland and Day were inspired by William Morris' Kelmscott Press and their books achieved a high standard of craftsmanship. The partnership continued until 1899.

In 1895 Day was elected a member of the Linked Ring and in 1898 held a successful one-man exhibition at the New York Camera Club. After instruction on photographic printing from his cousin Coburn in 1899, Day began to use processes other than platinum and to sign, instead of blind-stamping, his prints.

Day determined to show the standard of American photography to Europe and in 1900 travelled to London with Coburn. Stieglitz did not feel that Day's selection was fully representative of the American movement and instructed Horsley Hinton (for the Linked Ring) to refuse permission for this exhibition to be held at the Salon; however the RPS gave Day the use of their galleries. *The New School of American Photography* exhibition was a success, but it caused the rift between Day and Stieglitz, which probably led Day to refuse subsequent invitations to exhibit with the Photo-Secessionists or to be included in *Camera Work.*

Day continued to arrange semi-private exhibitions, including the 1902 *Portraits by a Few Leaders in the Newer Photographic Methods* and some of his early work was shown at the 1910 Albright Exhibition. In 1904 his studio was burned to the ground and his work lost. He retired from the public scene of photography and spent much of his time on his estate in Maine, where he continued to keep in contact with White.

After 1917 Holland Day's interest in photography declined. He never returned to Maine and chose to spend the rest of his life at Norwood, as a semi-invalid, until his death in 1933.

M. O. DELL 1883-1959

'Perfect portrayal of the moods of landscape' B. Sinkinson 1961

Mark Oliver Dell was born into a Quaker family in Walham Green, London and was educated at Sidcot School. He first became interested in photography in 1900 at the age of 17.

In 1905 he joined Hampshire House, where he was Secretary of the Trust and Workshops, devoting much of his time to the Hampshire House Photographic Society. By 1903 he was contributing to photographic exhibitions all over the world. He became a member of the RPS in 1915 and in 1921 was one of the founder members of the RPS Pictorial Group with J. C. Warburg, Agnes Warburg and Bertram Cox. After the closure of Hampshire House in 1923, he took up photography professionally and the following year was elected a Fellow of the RPS. The same year (1924) he joined in partnership with H. L. Wainwright; the results of their first commission for *Architectural Review* were artistically so much in advance of their contemporaries, that their work became in great demand by leading architects. During the early years of the partnership Dell also conducted photographic tours of the Pyrenees. At the end of 1926 Dell joined the BBC as a photographer, a post which he continued to hold until his retirement in 1945, when his partnership with Wainwright was also dissolved.

In 1956 Dell was elected an Honorary Fellow of the RPS for his contributions to pictorial and architectural photography. The following year he was invited to hold a one-man show at the RPS Galleries, in which he included

drawings and watercolours with his photographs. Also during 1957 he was elected to membership of the London Salon of Photography.

Dell was taken ill in the Pyrenees in 1959 and died later in England.

ROBERT DEMACHY 1859-1936

Leon Robert Demachy was born near Paris, the youngest child of Zoe Girod de l'Ain and Charles Adolphe Demachy, founder of the successful 'Banque Demachy'.

Demachy was a member of a wealthy family, and after being educated at a Jesuit School, and after a year as an army volunteer, he frequented artists' cafés in Paris. During the early 1880's he became increasingly interested in photography; in 1882 he was elected a member of the Société Francaise de Photographie.

In 1894 he started to make prints by the gum bichromate process and in 1895 was able to hold his first one-man show at the Photo-Club de Paris. During the following years he had prints exhibited at the RPS and published in *Camera Work.* He began experiments with Rawlin's oil process, which permitted more handwork on prints. In 1905 he was elected a member of the Linked Ring and an Honorary member of the RPS. Many of his photographs depict young girls portrayed in a romantic painterly style. He wrote extensively on the pigment processes in the photographic press. Other publications include illustrations for *Three Normandy Inns* (1910), '*Le Report des epreuves a l'huile* (1912) and *How to make Oil and Bromoil Prints in Monochrome and Colour* (1914).

Demachy gave up photography in 1914. His later life was spent at Hennequeville, near Trouville, where he died in 1936.

BARON A. DE MEYER 1868-1949

'The Debussy of Photography' Cecil Beaton

Adolf de Meyer was born in Paris of German-Jewish descent. His mother's maiden-name was Watson. He has been referred to as de Meyer-Watson and Von Meyer.

In 1897, a fashionable and elegant young man, he met Olga Caracciolo, god-daughter (reputedly daughter) of Edward VII, a professional beauty, and already model for Whistler, Conder and others. Adolf and Olga were married in 1899. In 1901, the year of his coronation, Edward VII arranged for de Meyer to be made a German Baron, so that he and Olga could attend this great occasion.

During the early 1900's the Baron was able to photograph the celebreties who visited his wife. In London the Baron was elected a member of the Linked Ring, where he exhibited from 1903. In New York in 1907, 1909 and again in 1912 de Meyer exhibited at Stieglitz' 291 Gallery, and subsequently a number of prints and gravures were published in *Camera Work* and *The Craftsman.*

In 1911 Diaghilev's company came to London and the de Meyers were involved with the organisation. The Baron photographed the ballet, resulting in the 1912 *Album of Photographic Studies* of Nijinsky and the other members of the company. In about 1912 Adolf and Olga travelled in Europe staying for some time in Venice. With the outbreak of war in 1914 the de Meyers, suspected of German connections, were forced to leave Britain for America. The Baron decided to earn his living as a professional photographer and was offered a generous contract by Condé Nast. Between 1914 and the early 1920's *Vogue* and *Vanity Fair* were dominated by de Meyer's elegant photographs. In 1923 he was contracted to *Harper's Bazaar* for 12 years.

The de Meyers returned to London. Olga remained chic, in spite of her addiction to morphine and heroin, which led to her death at the age of fifty-nine. The Baron moved to Paris, his contract with *Harper's Bazaar* was dissolved. The 2nd World War forced him to again leave for America, where he died alone in Hollywood.

R. DUHRKOOP 1848-1918

'The pioneer of artistic portrait photography on the Continent' Hoppé 1909

Rudolph Duhrkoop was born into a working family in Hamburg. He worked as a retail tradesman, except for a period in the army during the Franco-Prussian War in 1870 and 1871.

He became interested in photography in about 1880, and in 1883 gave up his job as a tradesman and opened a studio. At first he worked in the conventional manner of a portrait photographer, but he also attended art lectures, some of which were given by the art critic Lichwark, and visited exhibitions. By about 1886 he had abandoned taking portraits in a studio and had begun to use ordinary rooms, he would even go to the house of his sitter or photograph in the open air, ensuring that the figure predominated over the background. He no longer used gloss papers, preferring to print on a matt surface. In 1899 he exhibited fifty of these prints in Hamburg for which he received a gold medal and the highest award. More distinctions followed.

In 1900 Duhrkoop was sent by the town of Hamburg to the International Exhibition in Paris and in 1901 to London, where he was able to see the work of leading pictorialists. In 1904 he travelled to America to the St. Louis Exposition and visited the studios of several photographers, including Gertrude Kasebier. He began to exhibit his work outside Germany, and gained awards and notice at the major exhibitions, and in 1909 held a one-man show at the RPS. By this time he was operating two commercial studios, one in Hamburg and the other in Berlin, superintended alternately by himself and his daughter.

Duhrkoop died in Hamburg in 1918.

J. O. ECHAGUE 1886-

José Ortiz Echague was born in Guadajara, Spain. His father was the military engineer Antonio Ortiz Puertas and his mother Dolores Echague Santayo, daughter of the Count of Serrallo and he spent his early years in La Roija. He owned his first camera in 1898. In 1903 he made his first notable print, *Sermon en la Aldea* with the co-operation of the village people and priest.

Later in 1903 he began to study Military Engineering at the Academy in Guadajara. After the completion of his training he was appointed to the Expeditionary Force involved in the North African War. He returned to Spain in 1911, where he was commissioned as one of Spain's first aviators.

Echague had continued to take photographs and by 1906 had begun experimenting with pigment printing processes. He eventually developed his own process Carbondir (direct carbon). On his return to Spain in 1911 he started to record photophgraically the countryside, the architecture, the customs and the people. He exhibited his work first in the Spanish exhibitions and then internationally. In addition to European countries, Echague has exhibited in America, Mexico, South Africa and New Zealand. In England he has exhibited regularly at the London Salon; in 1933 he became a member of the RPS and in 1943 was elected to a Fellowship. Much of his photographic work has been published. He set up his own firm of publishers in order to maintain a high standard of reproduction. The first book *Espana: Tipos y Trajas* (*Local People and Costume*) appeared in 1930, *Espana: Pueblos y Paisajes* (*Villages and Landscape*) in 1938, *Espana: Mistca* (*Mysticism*) in 1943 and in 1971, *Espana: Castillos y Alcazares* (*Castles and Fortresses*).

Echague, now 91, is remembered not only for his continuing photographic achievements, but also for his positions in the aeronautical (CASA) and automobile (SEAT) industries.

(The authority in England on Echague is T. Herbert Jones FRPS.)

RUDOLF EICKEMEYER 1862-1932

Rudolf Eickemeyer was born in Yonkers, the son of the successful industrialist and inventor Rudolf Eickemeyer. In his early years he was interested in mechanics and sketching. After school he was apprenticed to a machinist, following which he was employed as a draughtsman in his father's machine factory. He was also able to travel extensively in North America.

In 1884 he bought his first camera and learned the photographic processes from a local portrait photographer. During the next ten years he took many photographs and began to exhibit his work. In 1893 he was invited to exhibit at the Hamburg Kunsthalle and was awarded a gold medal, and the following year received the Albert Medal at the RPS Salon. In 1895 he was elected to the Linked Ring Brotherhood and became a regular contributor to the Photographic Salon. In America, in 1900, he held his first one-man show at the New York Camera Club.

Eickemeyer's father died in 1895 and he became free to resign from his position in the firm, although he continued to act as Secretary for the Board. He then accepted an offer to work at the New York studios of James Breeze. In 1901 he moved to 590, Fifth Avenue and a position as Art Manager at the Cambell Art Studios. In 1905 he made another move to 249, Fifth Avenue to the Davis and Stanford Studio. Eickemeyer bought a half share in the firm, which later became Davis and Eickemeyer. Eickemeyer's work was reproduced in *Camera Work*, but he did not become a member of the Photo-Secession. Professionally Eickemeyer achieved success as a portrait photographer. In 1911 he was commissioned to photograph American ladies who had married into the British aristocracy. On his return to America he again joined the Cambell Studios, where he remained until 1915. He was elected to the London Salon in 1912; he held a retrospective exhibition at the Anderson Gallery in New York in 1922, shortly before his retirement.

Eickemeyer continued to travel and photograph. In 1929 he donated his collection to the Smithsonian Institute. He died in 1932, in Yonkers, after a long illness.

HUGO ERFURTH 1874-1948

Hugo Erfurth was born in Halle, Germany. He trained in Dresden at the Atelier Hoffert, following which he joined the studio of Schroder, the court photographer.

In 1904 he designed the special photographic section at the Dresden Exhibition. His photographic work, printed by the pigment processes of oil and gum, became internationally known; in England he was a member of the London Salon of Photography. Until the outbreak of the 1st World War he taught photography at the college of book production in Leipzig. In 1919 he founded the Society of German Photographers and was, for many years, its President. During the 1920's his Dresden studio became a meeting place for artists, many of whom he photographed.

Erfurth moved to Cologne in 1934, where during the 2nd World War many of his prints were destroyed, although a considerable amount of his work survived in a bank safe. He continued to photograph until his death in 1948 at Gaienhofen on Bodensee.

FRANK EUGENE 1865-1936

A talented worker who 'etches with a needle upon his negatives' Coburn 1901

Frank Eugene Smith was born in New York. He studied first at the City College of New York and after 1886, at the Royal Bavarian Academy of Fine Art in Munich.

Eugene was first recognised as a painter; he took up photography as a hobby. In London his work was exhibited at the 1899 Photographic Salon and he was elected to membership of the Linked Ring in 1900. In New York, in 1902 he was one of the 12 founder members of the Photo-Secession. He moved to Germany in 1906, but remained associated with the British and American photographic movements. He was an early exponent of the autochrome process and examples of his work, together with those of Steiglitz and Steichen were shown at the 291 Gallery in 1907. Selections of his prints reproduced in *Camera Work* were received with criticism and acclaim. He was a member of the controversial selection committee of the Linked Ring in 1908.

In Germany Eugene became successful as a teacher and in 1913 the Royal Academy of the Graphic Arts at Leipzig created a Chair in Photography and appointed him Professor of Pictorial Photography, the first academic recognition of this sort for photography.

Eugene died in 1936.

FREDERICK H. EVANS 1853-1943

'The greatest exponent of architectural photography' Stieglitz 1903

Frederick Henry Evans was born in Whitechapel, London, the son of Sarah (Barratt) and John Evans, a schoolmaster.

Frederick Evans kept a bookshop in the heart of the City of London, where he became acquainted with many notable literary personalities of the day. He dealt with many rare books including those from the William Morris Kelmscott Press, and he befriended the young illustrator Aubrey Beardsley.

Evans took up photography some time before 1886; in 1891 he exhibited a series of 'at home' portraits and in 1895 the portraits of a number of literary friends. In 1898 he gave up book-selling, married and retired to a cottage near Epping Forest, where he was able to devote more time to photography. His work became known in America when he exhibited in 1895 at Boston; he was the first British photographer to be represented by Stieglitz in *Camera Work* (1903) and later, in 1906, exhibited at '291'. In London he held his first one-man show at the RPS in 1900, where he met Coburn and Day, the same year he was elected a member of the Linked Ring.

Evans was particularly concerned with print presentation. He worked out a revolutionary scheme of arbitrary grouping for the hanging of the 1902 Salon, wrote a series of articles on mounting for the monthly *Photogram* magazine and in 1908 organised an exhibition of *Good and Bad Multiple Mounting*. When Evans began to work for *Country Life* in 1906, a change in his style became evident and in 1908 his prints, submitted for the Salon, were rejected. He joined the group of dissidents who rallied round F. J. Mortimer and his Salon des Refusés at the galleries of the *Amateur Photographer*.

Evans gave up photography after the 1st World War when platinum paper became unobtainable. In 1925 he was elected an Honorary Fellow of the RPS in recognition of his past contributions to photography. He died in London in 1944.

A. HORSLEY HINTON 1863-1906

Alfred Horsley Hinton was born in 1863. At school he showed an ability in drawing and painting; on Saturday afternoons, he was usually to be found at the studio of the artist John Peel, who encouraged him in his growing interest in art. He left school in about 1878 and spent the next year and a half continuing his painting studies.

In 1889 he started work in a warehouse in the City of London dealing with photographic materials; at weekends he escaped to Epping Forest to paint. During this time he became interested in photography and by 1890 had exhibited a few pictures which received favourable criticism. He was encouraged by several of the older photographers, notably H. P. Robinson, and also met his son Ralph.

Between 1888 and 1891 Horsley Hinton edited the short-lived *Photographic Art Journal*. In 1891 he was employed by Ralph Robinson to manage his Guildford Studios. Following which he devoted his energies to photographic journalism, especially in connection with the *Amateur Photographer*, which he had begun to edit in 1893. He continued as Editor of *Amateur Photographer*, until his death in 1908, writing extensively and doing much to popularise pictorial photography. A series on Landscape Photography, contributed by him, was first translated into French, then into German and finally published in book form. He also gave lectures on Pictorial Photography to societies and institutions. He was an early member of the Linked Ring and one of the original promoters of the Photographic Salon.

Horsley Hinton died suddenly at the age of 45, a few days after a visit to the Scottish Salon.

Th. AND O. HOFMEISTER c.1860's – 1943 & 1937

The production of 'wonderfully perfect landscapes' Ernst Juhl

Theodor Hofmeister and his younger brother Oscar were born in Hamburg in the 1860's. Theodor's early employment was as a wholesale merchant and Oscar was a Secretary of the County Court.

The Hofmeisters began their careers in photography in 1895 with the production of picture postcards. Between 1897 and 1899 they produced a large number of figure studies, depicting local people in their homes wearing traditional costume. The brothers would visit nearby picturesque areas and befriend the local people. Much care went into the production of a photograph, often the scene was first sketched by Theodor, and then he and Oscar would discuss the composition.

The Hofmeisters became members of Die Gesellschaft zur Forderung die Amateur Photographie, and first exhibited their work in Hamburg in 1897. In about 1902 they began to take pupils for instruction in photography and composition. In the Hofmeisters' later work the exposures were made by Oscar and the printing in gum was carried out by Theodor. By 1904 the work of the Hofmeisters was well known and acclaimed in Germany. They influenced and led the photographic club in Hamburg, and art institutes had begun to collect their work; these included the Kaiser Wilhelm Museum, the Dresden Kupferstichkabinette and the Hamburg Kunsthalle. Their prints were reproduced by Stieglitz in issue 7 of *Camera Work* and began to be exhibited internationally.

Oscar Hofmeister died in 1937 and Theodor in 1943.

E. O. HOPPE 1878-1972

Emil Otto Hoppé was born in Munich, the son of a banker. He was educated in Vienna and later joined his father's banking firm.

Around 1900 Hoppé arrived in England on the first stage of a journey to China. He decided to stay and took up a position with the Lombard Bank in London. In England he began to take photographs and met a number of photographers including J. C. Warburg, and became a member of the RPS (1903).

In 1907 he began his career in photography. He was elected a Fellow of the RPS and took over an artist's studio in Barons Court. He was a founding member of the London Salon of Photography in 1910 and held a one-man show at the RPS. His success as a portrait photographer was such that in 1913 he moved to a larger house and studio, Millais House, in South Kensington, where he remained until 1933.

In 1919 Hoppé travelled to America, the first of his many wanderings abroad. Soon after his return he gave up portraiture in favour of topographical views, although his book of *Fair Women* was not published until 1922. The photographs taken on his subsequent travels were published: the first *Gypsy*

Camp and Royal Palace: Wanderings in Rumania in 1924; *The Fifth Continent* (Australia) in 1931 and *Round the World with a Camera* in 1934. In 1945 he produced an autobiography entitled 100,000 *Exposures*.

Hoppé continued to photograph almost to the end of his life, an interview in 1968 showed him still lively and using a camera. He died in 1972 at the age of 94.

CHARLES JOB c.1853-1930

'An eminent photographer of pastoral landscape' *Practical Photographer* 1904

Charles Job was born in London. His artistic skills were developed early in his life, although his first employment, in 1870 was with a stockbroker.

Job took up photography in 1870, in the days of the wet plate. His interest was renewed in about 1880, and he joined the London Camera Club and was stimulated by the pictorial work of the members. He was then connected with the Postal Camera Club, to which Sutcliffe, Keighley and later Warburg belonged. The mutual print criticism provided by this organisation proved extremely interesting and helpful to him.

Job became a member of the RPS in 1893 and a Fellow in 1895. As an early exhibitor at the Photographic Salon he was elected to membership of the Linked Ring in 1900. With Horsley Hinton, he is said to have established a distinctly British School of Landscape Photography. For many years his brown carbon prints were shown at the international and other major exhibitions. During the next few years Job lived in various parts of the country; in Brighton and in Liverpool, where during the 1st World War he worked in the Censor Office. Finally he returned to London. In 1928, in recognition of his eminence in pictorial photography, he was awarded the distinction of Honorary Fellowship of the RPS.

In 1929 he moved to the South of France for health reasons, but with a further illness returned to London, where he died in 1929.

J. DUDLEY JOHNSTON 1868-1955

A Master of the Gum Platinum process.

J. Dudley Johnston was born in Liverpool in 1868. In 1883, at the age of fifteen, he began a career in commerce. He was interested in music and in art. His first experience with photography was in 1880, but he did not become a member of the Liverpool Photographic Society until 1904.

Dudley Johnston's early work was influenced by 'the romantic aspects of industrial cities'. He joined the RPS in 1907 and was also elected to membership of the Linked Ring. In 1908 four of his gum platinum prints were reproduced in *Studio* together with the work of other prominent pictorialists from Britain, Europe and America. He was President of the Liverpool Photographic Association between 1909 and 1911.

In 1911 business took Dudley Johnston to London, where he began his long involvement with the RPS. He served on the Council of the RPS from 1916 and was elected President in 1923. From 1923 until his death he was Curator of the Print Collection. He was a major force in the Pictorial Group and regularly hung the Annual Exhibition. He was elected Honorary Fellow in 1925 and received the distinction of a second duration as President between 1929-31. In the 1930's he turned his attention to landscape and mastered the delicate process of thiocarbamide transparencies. Dudley Johnston's many articles in the *Photographic Journal* give some indication of the depth of his research and his contribution to the history of the RPS and photography.

Dudley Johnston died in London in 1955.

GERTRUDE KASEBIER 1852-1934

Gertrude Stanton was born in Ohio, the daughter of American Quakers. She showed an early interest and ability in Art. On the death of her father, she moved to New York, where in 1874 she married Eduard Kasebier.

In 1888, at the age of thirty-six, she began to study painting at the Pratt Institute in Brooklyn. She then spent a short time in Paris and Germany to pursue her newer interest, photography. She returned to America and by 1897 had established a studio on Fifth Avenue, where she became successful as a portrait photographer. In New York she met Stieglitz and had her first exhibition at the Camera Club. She was a founding member of the Photo-Secession and a member of the Linked Ring. In 1903 her work was illustrated in the first issue of *Camera Work*. During the first part of the century Kasebier's work was shown at the major photographic exhibitions on both sides of the Atlantic. She photographed many eminent personalities and illustrated books.

After the 1910 Albright Exhibition at Buffalo, Kasebier continued working in the pictorial style. She broke with Stieglitz and '291', and in 1915 with White and Coburn founded Pictorial Photographers of America. She continued to photograph and last exhibited at the Brooklyn Institute in 1926. She retired from her studio in 1927.

Gertrude Kasebier died at her home in New York in 1934.

C. DAVID KAY c.1880's-?

C. David Kay was born in Perthshire, the son of the Rev. C. D. Kay D.D. As a young man he spent several holidays in the Alps, in the company of his elder brother, W. R. Kay, whose work in pictorial photography also received recognition.

The Kays first exhibited at the RPS in 1904, and during the next few years David Kay's prints, primarily made using pigment processes, began to receive recognition. In 1910 he was described as 'another young worker making a brave show' at the RPS Exhibition and later as 'the youngest member of the London Salon'.

After 1912 mention of his work ceased and a later mention in the photographic press described his death as 'untimely'.

ALEX KEIGHLEY 1861-1947

'One of the most eminent pictorial photographers' Dudley Johnston 1947

Alexander Keighley was born in Keighley, Yorkshire, the younger son of a successful textile manufacturer. Early in Alexander's life the family moved the short distance to Steeton and a C17 manor house. Alexander attended the local Trade and Grammar School, where at 15, he became Head Boy. In 1877 he gained a scholarship to the Royal College of Science in South Kensington, London, where he was one of the youngest students. After graduation he entered his father's business, starting on the mill floor and working a twelve hour day.

From an early age Alex Keighley had sketched and painted. He was introduced to photography in about 1883 when he attended a local lecture, during which the use of the new dry plate was demonstrated. It inspired Keighley to buy a 'complete Stanton's Photographic outfit' and join the Bradford Photographic Society. Keighley's early attempts were influenced by the writing and work of H. P. Robinson; he first experimented with albumen and platinum and later with carbon, with which he was to work extensively.

In 1887, with a set of twelve prints, Keighley won a competition organised by the *Amateur Photographer* and in 1889 he exhibited at the RPS. The Linked Ring was founded in 1892 and Alex Keighley was invited to become a Member. He joined the RPS in 1910 and the following year was elected a

Fellow. During the next few years he exhibited in Britain and America and held a number of one-man shows in London, RPS (1910), Paris (1912), Vienna (1912), Munich (1913) and Washington (1917). The majority of his photographs were taken outside Britain.

In 1943 retrospective exhibitions of his work were held at Bradford Art Gallery and the RPS. Alex Keighley died in 1947.

HEINRICH KUEHN (KUHN) 1866-1944

'A vital force in the evolution of pictorial photography' *Camera Work* 1911

Heinrich Kuehn was born in Dresden in 1866. In about 1880, the young Kuehn, an asthma sufferer, chose the more suitable climate of Innsbruck for his medical studies. With other students, he frequented the Cafe Katzburg, and there met his future wife Emma Katzburg.

After completion of his medical studies Kuehn, who came from a wealthy family, was able to devote himself to his hobby, photography. Experiments with photographic processes and exhibitions led to contact with photographers Hugo Henneberg and Hans Watzeck, with whom he produced and published significant work. They formed 'Das Kleeblatt' or The Trifolium (their articles were signed with the cloverleaf), founded the German-Austrian school of photography and evolved the multiple gum printing method, so extensively used around the turn of the century.

In 1895 Kuehn was elected a member of the Linked Ring; the 13th issue of *Camera Work* published prints by the Trifolium, and following the important 1910 Buffalo Exhibition, in which Kuehn's work was included, the entire issue of *Camera Work* (No. 33) was devoted to him. In 1912 Kuehn founded a School of Photography in Innsbruck, which, with the development of the war, was disbanded in 1916.

Kuehn's wife died early, leaving him with three young children. He appointed an English governess, who stayed with the family until her death 48 years later; 'Miss Mary' appears in many of Kuehn's photographs. During the 1920's Kuehn began to work on lenses and produced the Kuehn Tieferbilden-Rodenstock-Imagon. Further developments included a movable-back camera, and in the 1930's work on a double emulsion film. In 1937 he was awarded an Honorary Doctorate of Philosophy at the University of Innsbruck, for his services to Scientific and Artistic aspects of Photography.

Kuehn died in 1944.

LEONARD MISONNE 1870-1943

A photographer of light and atmosphere.

Leonard Misonne was born in Gilly, Belgium, the youngest child of a lawyer. He studied engineering at the University of Lowen, and as a student became an enthusiastic amateur photographer. He graduated from university in 1895, but did not practice his profession; instead he devoted his time to the piano, painting and photography. Misonne was financially independant and able to travel extensively in Europe, including several visits to London

In 1896 Misonne, after a success in a photographic competition, decided to pursue the art of photography, and by 1900 had developed a distinctive style, in which light played a very important part. 'The theme is nothing in itself, light is all'. During the early 1900's he began to suffer from asthma, but continued his photography, which soon gained international recognition. He exhibited work in Belgium, France, Holland, America and in England, where he became a member of the London Salon. His photographs commonly depict small figures which form an integral part of a landscape, and up until 1915 were primarily made in carbon. After 1915 he changed to the oil process, which provided greater possibilities for manipulation of the print. He believed that some artificiality was justified to produce an artistic impression, and in an

article he wrote for the Belgium Photographic Society, describes a method of adding sky effects to landscape. After 1935 he started to work with the bromoil process.

In 1940 his health began to deteriorate; he died three years later.

F J. MORTIMER 1874-1944

'Unrivalled depictions of the ever changing moods of the ocean' Alex Keighley *Photographic Journal* 1944

Francis James Mortimer was born in Portsea, Portsmouth, the son of a dental surgeon. The family had many connections with the Scilly Isles. After leaving school Mortimer began to study Law, but soon transferred his interest to Journalism. In the 1880's Mortimer won a camera in a sketching competition and realised the possibilities of photography. His early work was very general and it was not until the early 1900's that he began to specialise in marine photography. Mortimer had little sympathy with brush work in the photographic print, although he admitted to printing in clouds and strengthening or reducing light, which adjustments were carried out on the negative.

Mortimer moved to London in 1904 to work on the staff of the *British Journal of Photography*, the same year he became a member of the RPS. The high standard of his pictorial work supported his election to Fellowship of the RPS in 1905 and membership of the Linked Ring in 1907. After the sudden death of Horsley Hinton in 1908 Mortimer began his long association with the *Amateur Photographer*; he was to edit this publication for thirty-six years. Mortimer was one of the factors instrumental in the break-up of the Linked Ring, when in 1908 he organised a *Salon des Refusés* at the Little Galleries of the *Amateur Photographer* in response to dissatisfaction over the selection of prints for the Photographic Salon of the Linked Ring. Subsequently, in 1910, the London Salon of Photography was established. As Editor of *Photograms of the Year* from 1912, he made a major contribution to the recording of international developments and progress in Pictorial Photography.

In 1932, in recognition of his service to Photographic Art and Journalism, an Honorary Fellowship of the RPS was conferred upon him. In 1938 he became Vice-President of the RPS and as President (1940-42), he succeeded in re-establishing friendly relations between the London Salon and the Royal Salon. His knowledge of photographic science and technique was of great use during the 2nd World War, and for his services he was awarded the CBE. He did much to revive the London Camera Club after the 1942 Blitz. In 1944 he was awarded the distinction of a Progress Medal, previously awarded by the RPS only to Emerson and Stieglitz for Pictorial Photography.

F. J. Mortimer died in London in 1944 as the result of injuries from a flying bomb.

WARD MUIR 1878-1927

'An important member in the small band of impressionists' *Practical Photographer* 1903

Wardrop Openshaw Muir was born in Derby, the son of the Rev. J. J. Muir, an expert microscopist, who was extremely skilful in scientific and botanical drawing. As a boy he was influenced by his father's skills and by his interest in impressionist painting. Muir suffered from a lung complaint and spent a considerable amount of time travelling abroad. He received some instruction from an Austrian artists and visited art galleries in Italy, France and Holland.

Ward Muir took up photography in about 1890, encouraged and helped by a friend. He continued to travel and began to write and photograph for the press. He was able to interpret a common subject in a new way and started to exhibit his work. His photographs were first shown at the Photographic Salon in 1901 and in 1904 he was elected to membership of the Linked Ring.

In a 1907 article Muir claimed his work to be influenced by decorative drawing in the German magazine *Jugend*. He exhibited at the RPS and was one of the early members of the new London Salon of Photography.

Muir became a major force in the Practical Correspondence College, an association for 'training photographers in the art of making the camera pay'. As a journalist, his work included novels and short stories, he also wrote regularly for the *Amateur Photographer* as 'the Bandit'. At the beginning of the 1st World War he enlisted with the Royal Army Medical Corps and during the war years edited their *Gazette*.

Ward Muir died in London in 1927.

HENRY RAVELL c.1860-1930

'Impresses one as work directly from the artists brush' Albright Gallery 1919

Henry Ravell was born in America and worked as an artist.

In about 1885 he travelled to Mexico, where he became the first artist to obtain any national recognition. He also used photography in his efforts to capture the vanishing way of Mexican life. In 1908 a number of his painterly gum prints were exhibited at the Thurber Gallery. In 1912, he and several other artists were commissioned by the Mexican Government to portray the country of Mexico, some of the resulting work was sent to America. In 1916 an article entitled 'Cathedrals of Mexico', illustrated by his work, was published in *Harper's* magazine. About this time he left Mexico, almost as a refugee. His studio in Cuernavaca was destroyed by rebels. He moved to California where he began to photograph near Carmel and settled at Santa Barbara. During 1919 his prints were exhibited at the Albright Gallery in Buffalo and at the Museum of History, Art and Science in Los Angeles. In *Century* magazine an article on 'Vanishing Mexico' was illustrated by his work.

Ravell died in the artists' colony at Santa Barbara in 1930.

GEORGE SEELEY 1880-1955

'Lyric quality in the Photo-Secessionist art' *Craftsman* 1907

George Seeley was born in Stockbridge, Massachusetts, he later studied Art in Boston.

Seeley's photographic work came into prominence in 1904, when his work was exhibited at the First American Salon. Coburn was one of the judges at this exhibition and was able to bring Seeley into contact with Stieglitz. Between 1906 and 1910 Seeley had nineteen photographs reproduced in *Camera Work* (issues 15, 20, 29).

Seeley continued his career as a painter and photographer, he became Supervisor of Art for the Stockbridge Schools and was also associated with the Stockbridge Congregational Church. He was an authority on birds and involved with the Biological Survey of Washington. Towards the end of his life Seeley became recognised as a still-life painter of brasses.

He died in Stockbridge in 1955.

EDWARD STEICHEN 1879-1973

Eduard (Edward) Steichen was born in Luxembourg in 1879. Two years later his parents emigrated to Michigan, where his father worked in the mines. He was educated at Milwaukee, where he showed considerable aptitude for Art. In 1894 he was apprenticed to a lithography company, but continued to study painting in his spare time.

He began to photograph in 1896, and by 1898 had prints accepted for the Philadelphia Photographic Salon. In 1899 his photographs were selected by White and Stieglitz for the exhibition at the Art Institute of Chicago, and by Holland Day for the *New School of American Photography* at the RPS Galleries in London (1900).

Later that year Steichen travelled to New York and sold a number of his photographs to Stieglitz.

Steichen was elected a member of the Linked Ring in 1901.

In Paris his paintings were accepted by the Salon of 1901 and the following year he held an exhibition of his paintings and photographs.

He returned to New York in 1902, contributed 14 prints to the first exhibition of the Photo-Secession, and took a studio at 291, Fifth Avenue, which on Stieglitz' instigation became 'The Little Galleries of the Photo-Secession'.

The 2nd issue of *Camera Work* illustrated Steichen's work; this was the first of many contributions.

In 1906 Steichen returned to France, when he became involved with a 'new' movement in art, and, as a result was able to send to Stieglitz work by Rodin, Marin, Weber, Cezanne, Picasso, Matisse, Brancusi and designer Gordon Craig. He remained in France with his wife Clara and family, involved with painting, photographing, and working with horticulture, until the outbreak of World War I.

When America entered the War Steichen was commissioned and worked as an advisor, and later in command of Aerial Photography.

He gave up painting after the War, when disillusioned by the appearance of one of his paintings, destroyed his work, and concentrated on photography, working for *Vogue* and *Vanity Fair*. In 1929 he organised the American section of the exhibition *Deutsche Werkbund* with Weston. Steichen retired in 1938, but with the outbreak of World War II commanded Navy Combat Photography, and directed two exhibitions at the Museum of Modern Art, *The Road to Victory* (1942) and *Power in the Pacific* (1945). He retired from the forces as Captain in 1946, and in 1947 was appointed Director, Department of Photography, Museum of Modern Art.

Steichen remained involved with photography until his death in 1973.

ALFRED STIEGLITZ 1864-1946

Alfred Stieglitz was born in Hoboken, New Jersey, the eldest child of Edward Stieglitz and Hedwig Werner. In 1881, after Edward Stieglitz's retirement from business, the family returned to Germany for a prolonged visit. Stieglitz studied at Karlsruhe and then Berlin, where he studied mechanical engineering. He bought his first camera in 1883 and transferred to Vogel's classes in Photochemistry, eventually abandoning engineering.

In 1887 Emerson awarded Stieglitz first prize in a competition organised by *Amateur Photographer*. He returned to America and in 1891 he joined the Society of Amateur Photographers, the following year he became editor of their publication. In 1894 he was invited to membership of the Linked Ring, after which he withdrew from business. Between 1897 and 1902 he edited *Camera Notes* the Journal of the Camera Club of New York, and organised numerous exhibitions. After his resignation as Editor of *Camera Notes*, he established *Camera Work*, the first issue of which appeared in 1903. Two years later, with the help of Steichen, he founded the Little Galleries of the Photo-Secession at 291, Fifth Avenue, where he showed many new and controversial photographs and paintings. The *International Exhibition of Photography*, the culmination of the achievements of the Photo-Secession, at the Albright Gallery in Buffalo, was organised by Stieglitz with the assistance of White, Weber and Haviland. Between 1915 and 1916 Stieglitz was involved with the proto-Dada publication *291*. In 1917 the last issue of *Camera Work* was printed and the '291' Gallery closed.

Stieglitz continued to photograph with increasing energy making the first pictures of his second wife, the painter, Georgia O'Keeffe, and at Lake George, his summer retreat, the series of Equivalents. In New York in 1925, he opened the Intimate Gallery, and in 1929 An American Place, where during

1932 and 1934 he held one-man shows of his photographs. In 1924 he was awarded the Progress Medal of the RPS (previously awarded only to Emerson for Pictorial Photography), the Townsend Harris Medal (1927), and the Honorary Fellowship of the Photographic Society of America (1940). In 1941 a selection of his photographs was acquired by the Museum of Modern Art and exhibited in 1942.

Stieglitz, whose health had been declining since 1937, died in New York in 1946.

PAUL STRAND 1890-1976

'The first advocate of a new realism in photography'

Paul Strand was born in New York City, of Bohemian descent. He was given his first camera at the age of 12. He studied photography under Lewis Hine, who also took him to visit the Gallery of the Photo-Secession at 291 Fifth Avenue.

In 1907 he decided to become a photographer and became a member of the New York Camera Club the following year. He frequently returned to '291' taking his work to Stieglitz for comment. In 1915 he began to make abstract photographs of common objects and 'really became a photographer'. Stieglitz organised a one-man show of his work in 1916 and devoted the last two issues of *Camera Work* to him.

From 1917, he spent three years in the Army, first as an X-ray technician and then as a medical film cameraman. In 1921 he made the avant-garde film *Manhattan* with Charles Sheeler and wrote articles on the work of O'Keeffe, Marin and Lachaise. By 1922 he had decided to move to Hollywood and earn his living as a freelance cinematographer. Following a visit to Maine, an exhibition of Strand's photographs of natural forms was shown at the Intimate Gallery (1928). 1929 was spent photographing in the Gaspe, from where he moved to New Mexico and in Mexico in 1933 he was appointed chief photographer and cinematographer for the Mexican Government. Here Strand produced the portfolio *Photographs of Mexico* (1940) and the civil rights film *Native Land* (1942). In 1945 the Museum of Modern Art held the Paul Strand retrospective. In 1950 he collaborated with Nancy Newhall on the publication *Time in New England*.

Strand went to live in France in 1948 where he continued to work with both still photography and motion pictures, and where he died in 1976.

KARL STRUSS 1887-

The cinematographer

Karl Fischer Struss was born in New York City, the youngest child of Henry Struss and Marie Fischer. He began photographing in 1896 with his elder brother's camera. In 1903, at 16, he was employed in his father's bonnet-wire factory, where he worked a ten hour day.

In 1908 his interest in photography had increased and he began to attend Clarence White's evening classes at Columbia University Teachers College. The following year he was able to spend ten weeks in Europe, during which time he took many of the images later to be exhibited in the 1910 Albright Exhibition at Buffalo and published in *Camera Work*. The same year, 1909, he devised his own single element lens, the 'Struss Pictorial Lens', which was successfully marketed. During the next few years he had a one-man show at Columbia and exhibited at the London Salon, the RPS, in Philadelphia and San Francisco, and with Clarence White was one of the founders of Pictorial Photographers of America.

Struss gave up employment at his father's factory in 1914 when he was commissioned by the Bermuda Government to produce tourist photographs and took over Clarence White's Studio on Fifth Avenue. Some of his photo-graphy from this period appeared in *Vogue*, *Harper's Bazaar* and *Vanity Fair*. He was also involved in processing and printing for de Meyer. His studio was across the street from '291' where Struss met and talked with Stieglitz. From 1917 Struss served in the 1st World War and his studio was taken over by his 'best friend' Paul Anderson.

After the War Struss moved to Hollywood, where he became a cameraman for Cecil B. De Mille. His success in this field has tended to overshadow his earlier attainments, although he continued to work with still photography and to exhibit his work.

Karl Struss retired in 1970.

AGNES WARBURG 1872-1953

'A pictorialist and colour photographer of great merit' Frank R. Newens

Agnes Beatrice Warburg was born in Kensington, London, the third of the five children of Frederick and Emma Warburg. She was educated at home by French and German governesses. She shared an interest in photography with her elder brother John Warburg, who had taken up photography in 1880.

Agnes Warburg's work was first exhibited at the Photographic Salon of the Linked Ring in 1900, and although her work continued to be shown right up to the last Salon in 1909, she did not become a member of the Linked Ring. Her work was exhibited at the newly founded London Salon, at the BPS and at the RPS, to which she was elected a member in 1916. She was a founder member of the Halcyon Womens Club (Art and Crafts Association) and an exhibition of her photographs was held there in 1914. She was an early worker in the autochrome and the Raydex processes (an early colour printing process and forerunner of Trichrome Carbro). In 1921 she was one of the founding members of the RPS Pictorial Group. Her home at Porchester Terrace became the meeting place for a group of early colour enthusiasts and led to the founding of the RPS Colour Group in 1927.

During the 2nd World War Agnes Warburg moved out of London to live in Minehead. She later settled in Surrey, where she presented part of Box Hill to the National Trust. She died in Surrey, at the age of 80.

J. C. WARBURG 1867-1931

'An impressionist in photography'

John Cimon Warburg was born in Paddington, London, the eldest son of a highly successful business man of Swedish-Jewish birth. From boyhood, John Warburg suffered from chronic asthma and was educated entirely at home. As a young man and until his marriage in 1898 his ill-health encouraged him to spend six months of the year with his aunt in Cannes in the South of France, the scene of many of his photographs.

J. C. Warburg took up photography in about 1880 and at first worked in the 'realist' style. As a man of independent means he was able to devote much of his time to photography, although he had a number of other interests – entomology, music and linguistics. His attention was first drawn to photography by Craig Annan's one-man show at the Camera Club. He joined the RPS in 1895 and became a member of the newly formed Postal Camera Club in 1899. This mutual print criticism group included the pictorialists Hoppé, F. J. Mortimer and later J. Dudley Johnston. Warburg wrote many articles for German and English publications and in 1903 a contribution to *Camera Work*. He worked chiefly with the platinum and gum processes and the autochrome process, when it was introduced commercially in 1907. Although Warburg's work was regularly shown at the Photographic Salon, he never became a member of the Linked Ring. In 1909 a contemporary source described him as 'one of the few British Pictorialists outside the Linked Ring who are seriously worth reckoning with'. Warburg was elected to the RPS

Council in 1913 and to Fellowship in 1916. He served on several committees and in 1921 was a founding member of the Pictorial Group.

J. C. Warburg died at his home in Kensington, London in 1931, after a long illness.

E. WARNER

E. Warner lived in North London. In 1906 several of his photographs were exhibited at the annual RPS Exhibition and in 1908 at the Photographic Salon of the Linked Ring. His work was reproduced in the special studio publication *Colour Photography* (see bibliography).

In December 1908 Stieglitz published an advance notice from '291' of an exhibition that was to take place the following year of the work of the progressive British workers W. Benington, M. Arbuthnot and E. Warner. This exhibition never took place.

J. B. B. WELLINGTON 1858-1939

'The front rank of Pictorial Workers' *Practical Photography* 1904

James Booker Blakemore Wellington was born in Lansdown, Bath in 1858. As a boy he showed abilities in science and engineering. His early training was in architecture, a career which he pursued only for a short time. He took up photography while still completing his studies, and from the beginning was interested in landscape. His work was concerned with light and shade, and in a 1904 article he claimed to be influenced by Constable, Gainsborough and Leader.

Wellington became a member of the RPS in 1887 and his work was regularly shown at the exhibitions. He was a member of the Hanging Committee for the controversial 1891 Exhibition, which led to the formation of the Linked Ring, to which he subsequently belonged. In 1890, in the early days of Kodak, Wellington was sent to America to train under George Eastman and in 1891 he became the first Manager of the new Kodak Works in Harrow. In America, Wellington had been urged to co-operate in fraudulent activities and although he had refused to participate, his knowledge of the scheme led to his resignation from Kodak in 1893. For a while he worked for Elliot and Sons, but then formed a partnership with his brother-in-law, H. H. Ward, in Elstree and developed the successful fast fine-grain Iso-Wellington photographic plate. The partnership of Wellington and Ward Ltd, continued until its amalgamation with Ilford. He was elected an Honorary Fellow of the RPS in 1935.

J. B. B. Wellington died at Elstree, Hertfordshire in 1939.

EDWARD WESTON 1886-1958

Edward Henry Weston was born in Highland Park, Illinois, the son of a doctor. Soon after his birth the family moved to Chicago. As a child Weston was rather frail. His mother died while he was young and he was mainly brought up by his sister. At school he enjoyed painting. At the age of 16 he was given a camera by his father. Weston was upset by the limitations of photography and in an attempt to overcome some of the difficulties began to read the photographic magazines. By 1903 he had saved enough money to buy a more versatile camera.

He started work as an errand boy with a wholesale company, gradually rising to salesman. In 1906 he travelled to California to visit his sister and took an unsuccessful job surveying for a railway. He married and in 1911, with help from his wife's parents, built a photographic studio and embarked on a course in photography. The studio was a success and his 'spontaneous' portraits acclaimed. In about 1912 he met the photographer Margarethe

Mather, who showed considerable interest in his work. In 1917 he was elected to membership of the London Salon, almost immediately he found himself involved in the reaction against pictorialism and in 1920 destroyed his old prizewinning negatives. In 1921 he met Tina Modotti and accompanied her to Mexico, where there was a market for his work. In Mexico he began writing his Daybooks, on which he continued to work until 1934.

Weston was the first photographer to be awarded a Guggenheim Fellowship (1937) after which the variety of his subject matter increased. In the early 1940's he became crippled with Parkinson's disease. His last photographs were made near Carmel, California in 1948. Edward Weston died at Carmel in 1958.

CLARENCE H. WHITE 1871-1925

Clarence Hudson White was born at West Carlisle, Ohio, the younger son of Lewis and Phoebe White. In 1887 the family moved to Newark, where after leaving school, Clarence White worked as a book-keeper for a grocery firm.

In 1893 Clarence White married Jane Felix and they visited the *World's Columbian Exposition* at Chicago, with its 'superabundance of Art'. Later that year White took up photography and, encouraged by his wife, spent much of his spare time taking photographs. In 1898, White was involved in the organisation of the Newark Camera Club, which was to become an influential force in photography; their first exhibition was held at the home of Emma Spencer. The same year, at the 1st Philadelphia Exhibition, White met F. Holland Day and Joseph Keiley. In 1899 White's work was shown at a number of exhibitions including the Linked Ring exhibition in London. He was elected to membership of the Linked Ring the following year.

White became increasingly involved in photography, gave up his employment and supported himself and his family by commercial photography, which demanded a certain amount of travelling. In 1905 White's prints were first reproduced in *Camera Work*. During the summer he and his family were invited to stay with F. Holland Day in Maine; this began White's long association with Maine. By 1906 the magnetic pull of the Photo-Secession and Stieglitz drew him to New York, where he opened a studio on Fifth Avenue, near '291'. During the autumn of 1907 White took over Arthur Dow's position in photography at Columbia University Teachers College. At the end of the year he collaborated with Stieglitz on a series of Nudes. He submitted work for the major exhibitions including the International Exhibition of Photography in Dresden and the 1910 Albright Exhibition at Buffalo.

The countryside of Maine continued to attract White. In 1910 he bought a house there and began a Summer School in Photography assisted by Day, Kasebier and Max Weber. Encouraged by this success he founded the Clarence White School of Photography in New York in 1914, where he taught, until his death, with assistance from Paul Anderson and an early pupil Karl Struss. Other students of Clarence White have included Bourke-White, Lange, Ulmann, Steiner, Outerbridge and Breuhl. In 1915 White was a major force in the founding of the Pictorial Photographers of America, although his own photography declined under a heavy teaching schedule.

White died suddenly during a trip to Mexico with some of his students. His School was continued by Mrs White and friends until 1943.

Biographies written by
Carolyn Bloore

BIBLIOGRAPHY

Alexander Keighley, Hon.FRPS: A Memorial; produced by the Pictorial Group of The Royal Photographic Society, London, 1947.

Amateur Photographer London 1884-

Anderson, A. J. *The Artistic Side of Photography in Theory and Practice* London, 1910; reprinted Arno Press, New York, 1973.

Anderson, Paul L. *The Fine Art of Photography* London, 1919; reprinted Arno Press, New York, 1973.

Artscanada: An inquiry into the aesthetics of photography December 1974.

Beaton, Cecil and Gail Buckland *The Magic Image: The Genius of Photography from 1839 to the Present Day* Weidenfeld and Nicolson, London, 1975.

Birmingham Photographic Society Journal 1905-1950.

British Journal of Photography Liverpool and London 1860-

Bry, Doris *Alfred Stieglitz: Photographer* Museum of Fine Arts, Boston, 1965.

Caffin, Charles H. *Photography as a Fine Art* New York, 1901; reprinted Morgan and Morgan, New York, 1971.

Camera Work New York 1903-1917.

Clattenburg, Ellen Fritz *The Photographic Work of F. Holland Day* Wellesley College Museum, Ma., 1975.

Cork, Richard *Vorticism and Abstract Art in the First Machine Age*; Vol. 1 and 2, Gordon Fraser, London, 1976.

Doty, Robert *Photo Secession, Photography as a Fine Art* Monograph No. 1, Rochester, New York; George Eastman House, 1960.

Echague, J. O. monograph produced by the Pictorial Group of The Royal Photographic Society.

Gernsheim, H. & A. (ed) *Alvin Langdon Coburn Photographer, an Autobiography* Faber and Faber, London, 1966.

Gernsheim, H. & A. (ed) *The History of Photography 1685-1914 from the camera obscura to the beginning of the modern era.* Thames and Hudson, revised edition, 1969.

Gillies, John Wallace *Principles of Pictorial Photography* New York 1923; reprinted Arno Press, New York, 1973.

Green, Jonathan (ed) *Camera Work: a Critical Anthology, Selections from the quarterly published by Alfred Stieglitz 1903-1917* Aperture, New York, 1974.

Guest, Anthony *Art and the Camera* London 1907; reprinted Arno Press, New York, 1973.

Harvith, Susan and John *Karl Struss; Man with a Camera*; Michigan, 1976.

Holme, Charles (ed) *Art in Photography* 'The Studio' London, 1905.

Holme, Charles (ed) *Colour Photography and Other Recent Developments of the Art of the Camera* 'The Studio', London, 1908.

Homer, William Innes *Alfred Stieglitz and the American Avant-Garde* Secker and Warburg, London, 1977.

Homer, William Innes (General Editor) *Symbolism of Light; The Photographs of Clarence H. White*; University of Delaware and Delaware Art Museum, 1977.

Heyman, Therese Thau *Anne Brigman, Pictorial Photographer/Pagan/Member of the Photo-Secession*; Oakland Museum, 1974.

Jay, Bill *Robert Demachy, Photographs and Essays* Academy Editions, London, 1974.

Julian, Philippe *De Meyer*; Thames and Hudson, London, 1976.

Lewis, S.; McQuaid, J.; Tait, D. *Photography: Source and Resource* Turnip Press, Pennsylvania, 1973.

Lloyd, Valerie *Photography: The First Eighty Years* Colnaghi, London, 1976.

Lyons, Nathan (ed) *Photographers on Photography* Prentice-Hall, New Jersey, 1966.

Naef, Weston *The Painterly Photograph* The Metropolitan Museum of Art, New York, 1973.

Newhall, Beaumont *Frederick H. Evans*, Aperture Inc., New York, 1973.

Newhall, Beaumont *The History of Photography from 1839 to the Present Day* Secker and Warburg, London, 1973.

Norman, Dorothy *Alfred Stieglitz: An American Seer* New York, 1973.

Photograms of the Year London 1895-1962.

Photographic Journal London 1853-

Photographic News London 1858-1908.

Photography and Focus London 1908-1918.

Madigan, Mary Jean *Photography of Rudolf Eikemeyer Jr.* Hudson River Museum, Yonkers, N.Y. 1972.

Pictorial Photography of J. Dudley Johnston 1905-1940 The Royal Photographic Society, London, 1947.

Robinson, H. P. *Pictorial Effect in Photography* London, 1869; reprinted Helios, Pawlet Vermont, 1971.

Robinson, H. P. *Picture-Making by Photography* 5th edition, London, 1897; reprinted Arno Press, New York, 1973.

Scharf, Aaron *Art and Photography* Allen Lane, The Penguin Press, London, 1968.

Scharf, Aaron *Pioneers of Photography* British Broadcasting Corporation, London, 1975.

Schwabik, M. and M. Misonne *Leonard Misonne, Ein Fotograf aus Belgien 1870-1943; Romantische Landschaft*, Seebruck am Chiemsee, 1976.

Sinkinson, Bertram *A Selection of the Pictorial Work of M. O. Dell*; produced by the Pictorial Group of The Royal Photographic Society, London, 1961.

Tilney, F. C. *The Principles of Photographic Pictorialism* Boston, 1930.

Wall, A. H. *Artistic Landscape Photography* London, 1896; reprinted Arno Press, New York, 1973.

GLOSSARY

Silver processes: glossy surfaces were not admired, but it was possible to obtain a matt or rough finish; the 'Platino-matt' bromide papers were recommended. Prints could be contact printed or enlarged.

Bromide: first produced by Peter Mawdsey in 1873; the paper is coated with a gelatin and silver bromide emulsion usually with a small addition of silver iodide. It gives a pure black print.

Chlorobromide: a similar paper; the emulsion contains silver bromide and silver chloride. It can produce a warm black to a warm brown or sepia coloured print, depending on the quantity of chloride or bromide and variations in processing.

Platinotype: a contact printing process invented by W. Willis in 1883. The emulsion does not include a colloid (e.g. gelatin) so the image formed from a platinum is in the paper fibres. A beautiful deep tonal range is produced and the image is permanent. Often described as platinum printing.

Palladiotype: was introduced c.1916 when the cost of platinum escalated during the 1st World War; the effect is similar to platinum and it is also capable of very delicate tone.

Pigment Processes: the pigment print was first introduced in 1855 by Poitevin in an attempt to devise a more stable alternative to silver prints. Prints were made on paper coated with gelatin mixed with pigment, and sensitised with potassium bichromate. When gelatin or gum arabic is sensitised with bichromate it hardens, and becomes insoluble when exposed to light.

Gum bichromate: paper is coated with gum, bichromate and a suitable pigment and contact printed from the negative. The exposed paper is then 'developed' in warm water, the light hardened pigmented shadows remain and the highlights are washed out.

Multiple Gum: the gum process is repeated two or three times, which permits intermediate modifications. Great care needs to be taken to keep the print in register.

Gum platinum: a second exposure made on a sensitised layer of gum, registered over an initial platinum print.

Carbon: Perfected by Joseph Swan in 1866 'Carbon Tissue' is ready coated with gelatin and pigment and is sensitised before use with bichromate. It is contact printed from the negative and after exposure is soaked and then pressed into contact with transfer paper. After a second soaking in warm water the tissue is peeled off, leaving the picture adhering to the transfer paper. Soluble, unhardened gelatine is washed away.

Oil: Introduced by Rawlins in 1904 the negative is contact printed from a sensitised gelatin emulsion and after exposure is immersed in water, so that the unexposed, unhardened areas swell and become waterlogged. Oil pigment applied with a brush, is rejected by the swollen areas and accepted by the hardened gelatin.

Bromoil: a Bromide paper is exposed to the negative by contact or enlargement. The paper is then bleached to remove the blackened silver but leaves the image in a condition which will take up oil pigment applied with a brush.

Bromoil transfer: An impression from an inked bromoil image can be transferred, under pressure, to another paper.

Photogravure: this process was invented by Karl Klic in 1895, although Fox Talbot's Photoglyphic Engraving of 1852 was similar. A negative image produced on Carbon Tissue, sensitised with bichromate, is transferred to a copper plate or cylinder. The unhardened gelatin is washed away and the dried plate etched. The depth of the image varies with the thickness of the gelatin; this corresponds to the tonal range of the image. The etched image is inked, the plate wiped clean and printed under pressure.

Autochrome: developed in 1903 by Auguste and Louis Lumiere and introduced commercially in 1907. Starch grains, dyed in the 3 primary colours, were coated onto a glass plate to form a 'colour screen'. A panchromatic emulsion was laid over the top. The exposure was made through the colour screen, and after reversal development, viewed through the same screen.

SELECTED BIBLIOGRAPHY OF NON-SILVER PROCESSES

Blanchard, V. *Carbon or Pigment Printing* 1893
Wall, E. J. *Carbon Printing* 1894
Sawyer, J. R. *The ABC Guide to autotype Carbon Printing* 1909
Maskell, A. & Demachy, R. *Photo Aquatint or Gum Bichromate Process* 1897
Demachy, R. *The Rawlins Process*
Mortimer, F. J. & Coulthurst, S. L. *The Oil and Bromoil Processes* 1909
Hinton, A. H. *Platinotype Printing* 1897
Platinotype Co. *The Platinotype Process* 1885
Huson, Thos. *Photo-aquatint and Photogravure* 1897
Wilkinson, W. T. *Photogravure* 1890

CATALOGUE OF EXHIBITS

JOHN H. ANDERSON

1
Lower Thames Street 1913
Photogravure 240 x 180 mm
The Royal Photographic Society

2
Trawlers 1913 (Plate 8)
Photogravure 205 x 270 mm
The Royal Photographic Society

3
Thames off Wapping 1914
Photogravure 135 mm x 200 mm
The Royal Photographic Society

4
The White Sail c.1920 (Plate 10)
Photogravure 260 x 220 mm
The Royal Photographic Society

J. CRAIG ANNAN

5
The Riva, Schiavoni 1896
Photogravure 110 x 145 mm
The Royal Photographic Society

6
The White House 1905 (Plate 34)
Photogravure 253 x 234 mm
T. & R. Annan & Sons Ltd

7
The Thames near Henley 1908
Photogravure 209 x 361 mm
T. & R. Annan & Sons Ltd

8
Bolney Backwater 1908
Photogravure 215 x 278 mm
T. & R. Annan & Sons Ltd

9
Bullock Cart, Burgos 1913 (Plate 19)
Photogravure 140 x 170 mm
The Royal Photographic Society

MALCOLM ARBUTHNOT

10
To Larboard c.1907 (Plate 9)
Oil pigment process print 190 x 230 mm
The Royal Photographic Society

11
La Laveuse 1909
Gum platinum print 345 x 280 mm
The Royal Photographic Society

12
Reflections 1909 (Plate 5)
Gum platinum print 325 x 265 mm
The Royal Photographic Society

13
By the Sea 1910 (Plate 4)
Platinum print 337 x 218 mm
The Royal Photographic Society

J. C. BATKIN

14
Edinburgh View c.1900
Gum bichromate print 370 x 480 mm
Birmingham Photographic Society

15
Thames and Tower Bridge c.1900
Gum bichromate print 380 x 480 mm
Birmingham Photographic Society

16
A Rift in the Fog 1906
Gum bichromate print 210 x 340 mm
The Royal Photographic Society

17
Whilst the Daylight lasts 1908 (Plate 21)
Multi-gum bichromate print 450 x 350 mm
The Royal Photographic Society

WALTER BENINGTON

18
Among the Housetops 1900 (Plate 1)
Gum bichromate print 240 x 350 mm
The Royal Photographic Society

19
After the Storm 1903 (Plate 25)
Gum bichromate print 490 x 280 mm
The Royal Photographic Society

20
The Church of England 1903
Platinum print 195 x 145 mm
The Royal Photographic Society

ANNIE BRIGMAN

21
Spirit of the Glacier 1906
Platinum print 230 x 130 mm
The Royal Photographic Society

22
Spirit of Photography 1908
Platinum print 190 mm diameter
The Royal Photographic Society

A. L. COBURN

23
F. Holland Day 1900
Gum platinum print 290 x 180 mm
The Royal Photographic Society

24
Self Portrait 1905
Platinum print 220 x 250 mm
The Royal Photographic Society

25
New York, Stock Exchange 1900/10 (Fig. 12)
Photogravure 245 x 180 mm
The Royal Photographic Society

26
New York, Tunnelers 1900/10 (Plate 23)
Photogravure 260 x 210 mm
The Royal Photographic Society

27
Trafalgar Square 1905/10
Photogravure 210 x 160 mm
The Royal Photographic Society

28
Wapping 1905/10 (Plate 2)
Photogravure 210 x 160 mm
The Royal Photographic Society

29
'Spider's Web' - Liverpool 1906 (Plate 6)
Gum platinum print 360 x 250 mm
The Royal Photographic Society

30
Portrait of G. B. Shaw 1908 (Frontispiece)
Modern reproduction from original autochrome
200 x 144 mm
The Royal Photographic Society

31
Kingsway 1910 (Fig. 13)
Photogravure 220 x 110 mm
The Royal Photographic Society

32
The Great Temple, Grand Canyon 1911 (Fig. 7)
Gum platinum print 420 x 620 mm
The Royal Photographic Society

33
Vortograph No. 8 1916
Bromide print 290 x 210 mm
The Royal Photographic Society

34
Vortograph of Ezra Pound 1917 (Fig. 20)
Bromide print 283 x 199 mm
International Museum of Photography at George
Eastman House

GEORGE DAVISON

35
Ring Horses 1898
Photogravure on satin 90 x 115 mm
The Kodak Museum

36
The Long Arm 1900 (Plate 11)
Photogravure 115 x 165 mm
The Kodak Museum

37
Landscape c.1905
Photogravure 150 x 255 mm
The Kodak Museum

38
Near Portmadoc c.1905
Photogravure 160 x 245 mm
The Kodak Museum

F. HOLLAND DAY

39
Nude Boy (à la Flandrin) 1900
Platinum print 115 x 155 mm
The Royal Photographic Society

40
Nude with Trumpet c.1900
Platinum print 162 mm diameter
The Royal Photographic Society

41
A Marine 1910
Platinum print 187 x 230 mm
The Royal Photographic Society

42
Nude in Shadow 1910
Platinum print 240 x 190 mm
The Royal Photographic Society

M. O. DELL

43
Father Thames 1914
Bromide print 270 x 450 mm
The Royal Photographic Society

44
Whitchurch c.1916
Bromide print 240 x 450 mm
The Royal Photographic Society

ROBERT DEMACHY

45
Decorative Study in Red 1898
Gum bichromate print 150 mm diameter
The Royal Photographic Society

46
A Study in Red c.1898
Photogravure 169 x 123 mm
International Museum of Photography at George
Eastman House

47
Behind the Scenes 1900
Gum bichromate print 190 x 115 mm
The Royal Photographic Society

48
Sur le Grève 1907 (Plate 7)
Gum bichromate print 150 x 210 mm
The Royal Photographic Society

R. DUHRKOOP

49
Clothilde von Derp 1913 (Plate 29)
Gum bichromate print 270 x 220 mm
The Royal Photographic Society

J. O. ECHAGUE

50
Moro al Viento 1909 (Plate 31)
Fresson process print 222 x 168 mm
T. Herbert Jones Collection

51
Tetuan el Santon 1913
Fresson process print 235 x 149 mm
T. Herbert Jones Collection

RUDOLF EICKEMEYER

52
Close of an Autumn Day 1908
Bromide print 350 x 276 mm
Smithsonian Institution

53
The Lily Pond at Early Morning 1911
Bromide print 340 x 455 mm
Smithsonian Institution

54
A Morning in June on the Sawmill River
Yonkers 1908
Carbon print 238 x 191 mm
Smithsonian Institution

HUGO ERFURTH

55
Das Mädchen 1910
Gum bichromate print 210 x 330 mm
The Royal Photographic Society

FRANK EUGENE

56
Rebecca 1901 (Plate 32)
Platinum print 160 x 120 mm
The Royal Photographic Society

57
A Profile (Miss G.) 1908
Platinum print 170 x 120 mm
The Royal Photographic Society

58
HRH Prince Luitpold of Bavaria 1908
Platinum print 170 x 120 mm
The Royal Photographic Society

59
Nude 1908
Platinum print 170 x 120 mm
The Royal Photographic Society

60
The Horse c.1908 (Plate 20)
Photogravure 90 x 120 mm
The Royal Photographic Society

FREDERICK H. EVANS

61
Ely. A Memory of the Normans 1899
Platinum print 200 x 130 mm
The Royal Photographic Society

62
F. H. Day in Algerian Costume c.1901 (Plate 27)
Platinum print 237 x 120 mm
International Museum of Photography at George
Eastman House

63
York Minster – Into the South Transept 1902
Platinum print 210 x 130 mm
The Royal Photographic Society

64
On the Road to Watendlath: Borrowdale 1904
Platinum print 111 x 70 mm
International Museum of Photography at George
Eastman House

65
Westminster Abbey No. 26 – The Transepts,
South to North 1911
Platinum print 240 x 170 mm
The Royal Photographic Society

66
Westminster Abbey No. 27 1911
Platinum print 240 x 190 mm
The Royal Photographic Society

A. HORSLEY HINTON

67
Weeds and Rushes 1902 (Fig. 5)
Photogravure 200 x 170 mm
The Royal Photographic Society

68
Fleeting and Far 1903 (Plate 14)
Photogravure 205 x 160 mm
The Royal Photographic Society

69
St. Louis 1904
Platinum print 370 x 500 mm
The Royal Photographic Society

TH. AND O. HOFMEISTER

70
Haymaker 1899
Gum bichromate print 430 x 590 mm
The Royal Photographic Society

71
Solitary Horseman 1900 (Plate 12)
Photogravure 130 x 180 mm
The Royal Photographic Society

E. O. HOPPE

72
Portrait of a Lady 1909
Carbon print 200 x 150 mm
The Royal Photographic Society

73
Portrait of A. P. Allinson c.1909 (Plate 33)
Chlorobromide print 154 x 108 mm
The Royal Photographic Society

74
Sir Jacob Epstein in front of Oscar Wilde's
Memorial 1912
Platinum print 154 x 108 mm
The Mansell Collection

CHARLES JOB

75
Morning Mist on Sussex Downs 1905 (Plate 17)
Carbon print 260 x 350 mm
The Royal Photographic Society

76
Burning Leaves, Kensington Gardens 1920
Carbon print 260 x 350 mm
The Royal Photographic Society

77
Canal at Sluys
Carbon print 220 x 280 mm

The Royal Photographic Society

J. DUDLEY JOHNSTON

78
Manchester – River Medlock 1906 (Fig. 6)
Gum platinum print 360 x 280 mm
The Royal Photographic Society

79
Liverpool – An Impression 1907 (Plate 3)
Gum bichromate print 360 x 220 mm
The Royal Photographic Society

80
Snow in the City – Birmingham 1908
Gum platinum print
The Royal Photographic Society

81
Valley of the Dragon 1909
Gum platinum print 270 x 360 mm
The Royal Photographic Society

82
Corfe Castle 1910 (Plate 15)
Gum platinum print 250 x 360 mm
The Royal Photographic Society

83
Edinburgh – Dawn 1911
Gum platinum print 230 x 350 mm
The Royal Photographic Society

GERTRUDE KASEBIER

84
Happy Days c.1905
Platinum print 203 x 152 mm
Lunn Gallery/Graphics International Ltd

85
'The Rehearsal', John Murray Anderson Dance
Company
Platinum print 229 x 300 mm
International Museum of Photography at George
Eastman House

86
Turner Family, Woburn, Mass.
Platinum print 107 x 232 mm
International Museum of Photography at George
Eastman House

87
Untitled (Clarence White's son leaning on a wall)
(Plate 35)
Platinum print 342 x 257 mm
The Museum of Modern Art, New York. Gift of
Miss Mina Turner

88
Untitled (Profile of a Woman)
Fresson process print 259 x 200 mm
The Royal Photographic Society

C. DAVID KAY

89
Sunset at Blois c.1911
Bromoil print 260 x 320 mm
The Royal Photographic Society

90
Thames Morning Kew 1912
Bromoil print 260 x 190 mm
The Royal Photographic Society

ALEX. KEIGHLEY

91
Grace before Meat 1901
Carbon print 350 x 480 mm
The Royal Photographic Society

92
Adieu 1903
Carbon print 290 x 360 mm
The Royal Photographic Society

93
Bridge 1906
Carbon print 380 x 540 mm
The Royal Photographic Society

94
Fantasy 1915 (Plate 18)
Carbon print 400 x 570 mm
The Royal Photographic Society

HEINRICH KUEHN

95
Portrait of a Girl c.1900
Photogravure 260 x 240 mm
The Royal Photographic Society

96
Untitled (Girl stoops)
Platinum print on rice paper 232 x 292 mm
International Museum of Photography at George
Eastman House

97
Untitled (Woman in riding habit) (Plate 28)
Oil transfer print 380 x 265 mm
International Museum of Photography at George
Eastman House

98
Untitled (Team ploughing)
Oil transfer print 320 x 413 mm
International Museum of Photography at George
Eastman House

99
Untitled (Children in blue)
Modern reproduction from original Autochrome
160 x 135 mm
International Museum of Photography at George
Eastman House

100
Untitled (Girls crossing fields)
Modern reproduction from original Autochrome
130 x 158 mm
International Museum of Photography at George
Eastman House

BARON A. DE MEYER

101
Untitled (Olga de Meyer with chairs) c.1900
Platinum print 250 x 187 mm
IMP-GEH, Louise Dahl Wolfe Collection

102
Untitled (Olga de Meyer with parasol) c.1900
(Plate 37)
Platinum print 224 x 160 mm
IMP-GEH, Louise Dahl Wolfe Collection

103
Waterlilies 1907
Platinum print 260 x 350 mm
The Royal Photographic Society

104
Miss Heather Firbank c.1907
Platinum print 231 x 180 mm
Victoria and Albert Museum

105
Hydrangea 1908
Platinum print 330 x 270 mm
The Royal Photographic Society

106
Untitled c.1908
Modern reproduction from original autochrome
The Royal Photographic Society

107
Marchesa Casati 1912
Photogravure on Japan tissue 219 x 163 mm
Christopher Wood

108
From the Shores of the Bosphorus c.1912
Photogravure from Camerawork Vol. 40 1912
238 x 159 mm
Lunn Gallery/Graphics International Ltd.

LEONARD MISONNE

109
Automne c.1920

Bromoil print 290 x 390 mm
The Royal Photographic Society

F. J. MORTIMER

110
The Wreck (The Trail of the Hun) 1916
Bromoil print 390 x 390 mm
The Royal Photographic Society

111
The Gate of Goodbye 1917
Carbon print 340 x 480 mm
The Royal Photographic Society

112
The Gate of Goodbye (Separation 1) 1917
Carbon print 287 x 230 mm
The Camera Club Permanent Collection

113
The Gate of Goodbye (Separation 2) 1917
Carbon print 205 x 184 mm
The Camera Club Permanent Collection

114
Minesweeper All's Well 1917
Bromoil print 350 x 450 mm
The Royal Photographic Society

115
The End of the Trail 1919
Bromoil print 340 x 485 mm
The Camera Club Permanent Collection

WARD MUIR

116
An American Impression, the Bridge below
Niagara 1913
Platinum print 190 x 222 mm
The Royal Photographic Society

117
Lake District Landscape 1916
Carbon print 360 x 285 mm
The Royal Photographic Society

GEORGE SEELEY

118
Glowworm 1903/08
Platinum print 240 x 190 mm
The Royal Photographic Society

119
Untitled c.1908
Platinum print 240 x 190 mm
The Royal Photographic Society

EDWARD STEICHEN

120
The Pool 1899 (Plate 13)
Platinum print 200 x 150 mm
The Royal Photographic Society

121
Time Space Continuum 1920
Two-colour photograph 345 x 423 mm
The Museum of Modern Art, New York. Gift of
the photographer

122
F. H. Evans
Platinum print 210 x 170 mm
The Royal Photographic Society

123
Cyclamen – Mrs Philip Lydig
Photogravure from Camerawork Vol 42/3 1913
194 x 159 mm
Lunn Gallery/Graphics International Ltd

124
Steeplechase Day, Paris: After the Races
Duogravure from Camerawork Vol. 42/3 1913
159 x 197 mm
Lunn Gallery/Graphics International Ltd.

ALFRED STEIGLITZ

125
Hand of Man 1902
Photogravure 310 x 260 mm
The Royal Photographic Society

126
In New York Central Yards 1904
Photogravure 310 x 260 mm
The Royal Photographic Society

127
Going to the Post 1904 (Plate 24)
Photogravure 210 x 190 mm
The Royal Photographic Society

128
Untitled (Woman with a red flower)
Modern reproduction from original Autochrome
152 x 111 mm
International Museum of Photography at George
Eastman House

PAUL STRAND

129
Snow in Backyard, New York 1915
Photogravure from Camerawork, No. 48, 1916
345 x 423 mm
The Museum of Modern Art, New York

130
Bowls and Apples, Twin Lakes, Conn. 1915
Bromide print 248 x 317 mm
The Estate of Paul Strand and Hazel Strand

131
Telegraph Poles 1916 (Plate 26)
Photogravure from *Camerawork*, Vol. 48 1916
200 x 140 mm
Lunn Gallery/Graphics International Ltd.

132
Man, looking up, New York 1916
Bromide print 280 x 254 mm
The Estate of Paul Strand and Hazel Strand

133
Truckman's House, New York 1920
Bromide print 254 x 203 mm
The Estate of Paul Strand and Hazel Strand

KARL STRUSS

134
The Balcony, Sorrento exposed 1909, printed 1910
Hand-coated multiple platinum print (four printings) 140 x 190 mm
Karl and Ethel Struss

135
Metropolitan Life Insurance Tower, New York exposed 1909, printed 1912
Hand-coated sepia-toned multiple platinum print 63 x 38 mm
Karl and Ethel Struss

136
Lower Broadway, New York 1912
Bromide print on commercial bromide 'Japanese tissue paper' 330 x 254 mm
Karl and Ethel Struss

137
Brooklyn Bridge, Nocturne c.1913
Platinum print 95 x 114 mm
Karl and Ethel Struss

138
Fifth Avenue, Twilight, New York c.1914/15
Platinum print 305 x 235 mm
Karl and Ethel Struss

139
The Claremont Inn, Riverside Drive, New York 1915
Gelatin silver print 265 x 318 mm
The Metropolitan Museum of Art, New York

J. C. WARBURG

140
The House on the Marsh 1903
Gum bichromate print 555 x 400 mm
The Royal Photographic Society

141
Farm c.1903
Gum bichromate 150 x 100 mm
The Royal Photographic Society

142
Rushy Shore, Seaton 1907 (Plate 16)
Gum bichromate print 150 x 105 mm
The Royal Photographic Society

143
Cow on Saltburn Sands c.1910
Modern reproduction from original autochrome
111 x 155 mm
The Royal Photographic Society

144
Peggy under fruit trees c.1910
Modern reproduction from original autochrome
155 x 111 mm
The Royal Photographic Society

145
Peggy reading, seated c.1910
Modern reproduction from original autochrome
155 x 111 mm
The Royal Photographic Society

AGNES WARBURG

146
J. C. Warburg in Darkroom
Platinum print 195 x 140 mm
Miss Joan Warburg

E. WARNER

147
The Witches Tree 1908
Multi-gum bichromate print
The Royal Photographic Society

148
Navvies 1908 (Plate 22)
Multi-gum bichromate print 310 x 220 mm
The Royal Photographic Society

J. B. B. WELLINGTON

149
The Letter 1914
Bromide print 290 x 285 mm
The Royal Photographic Society

150
Refreshing Moments 1915
Bromide print 330 x 260 mm
The Royal Photographic Society

151
Mother's Jewels 1917 (Plate 30)
Bromide print 225 x 365 mm
The Royal Photographic Society

EDWARD WESTON

152
Margrethe with Fan 1914
Platinum print 235 x 160 mm
Dody W. Thompson, Los Angeles

153
Maude Allen 1915
Platinum print 407 x 283 mm
Barbara Kasten & Leland Rice, Inglewood, California

154
Bathing Pool 1919
Platinum print 240 x 190 mm
Collection of Oakland Museum, gift of Dr and Mrs Dudley P. Bell

CLARENCE WHITE

155
Blind Man's Buff 1899
Platinum print 185 x 135 mm
The Royal Photographic Society

156
The Cave 1901 (Plate 36)
Platinum print 233 x 181 mm
The Museum of Modern Art, New York. Mrs Douglas Auchincloss Fund

157
The Kiss 1904
Platinum print 244 x 145 mm
The Museum of Modern Art, New York. Extended loan from the Estate of Lewis F. White

158
The Mirror 1912
Platinum print 245 x 189 mm
The Museum of Modern Art, New York. Gift of Mrs Willard Helburn

REPRODUCTION CREDITS

T. and R. Annan & Sons Limited, Glasgow.
Plate 34

International Museum of Photography at George Eastman House, Rochester, N.Y.
Figss. 2, 8, 10, 11, 14, 15, 16, 18, 20
Plates 27, 28, 37, 38

T. Herbert Jones Collection, London.
Plate 31

Kodak Museum, Harrow.
Plate 11

Metropolitan Museum of Art, New York.
Fig. 17

Metropolitan Museum of Art, The Alfred Stieglitz Collection, 1949.
Fig. 1

Museum of Modern Art, New York
Plate 35, 36

The Royal Photographic Society, London
Figs. 5, 6, 7, 9, 12, 13, 19
Plates. Frontispiece, 1, 2, 3, 4, 5, 6, 7, 8, 9, 10, 12, 13, 14, 15, 16, 17, 18, 19, 20, 21, 22, 23, 24, 25, 26, 29, 30, 32, 33, 40.

The Witkin Gallery Inc., New York.
Plate 39

LENDERS

T. and R. Annan & Sons Ltd, Glasgow 6, 7, 8

Birmingham Photographic Society 14, 15

The Camera Club Permanent Collection, London 112, 113, 115

International Museum of Photography at George Eastman House, Rochester, N.Y. 34, 46, 62, 64, 85, 86, 96, 97, 98, 99, 100, 101, 102, 128

T. Herbert Jones, London 50, 51

Barbara Kasten and Leland Rice, California 153

The Kodak Museum, Harrow 35, 36, 37, 38

Lunn Gallery/Graphics International Ltd, Washington 84, 108, 123, 124, 131

The Mansell Collection, London 74

The Metropolitan Museum of Art, New York 139

The Museum of Modern Art, New York 87, 121, 129, 156, 157, 158

Oakland Museum, California 154

The Royal Photographic Society, London 1, 2, 3, 4, 5, 9, 10, 11, 12, 13, 16, 17, 18, 19, 20, 21, 22, 23, 24, 25, 26, 27, 28, 29, 30, 31, 32, 33, 39, 40, 41, 42, 43, 44, 45, 47, 48, 49, 55, 56, 57, 58, 59, 60, 61, 63, 65, 66, 67, 68, 69, 70, 71, 72, 73, 75, 76, 77, 78, 79, 80, 81, 82, 83, 88, 89, 90, 91, 92, 93, 94, 95, 103, 105, 106, 109, 110, 111, 114, 116, 117, 118, 119, 120, 122, 125, 126, 127, 140, 141, 142, 143, 144, 145, 147, 148, 149, 150, 151, 155

Smithsonian Institution, Washington 52, 53, 54

The Estate of Paul Strand and Hazel Strand 130, 132, 133

Karl and Ethel Struss 134, 135, 136, 137, 138

Dody W. Thompson, California 152

Victoria and Albert Museum, London 104

Miss Joan Warburg, London 146

Christopher Wood, London 107

INDEX

The entries in this index are given in the following order—page number of references in the text; page numbers of illustrations in the text (prefixed Illustrations); Plate numbers of the duotone reproductions; number of the catalogue entry to be found on pages 88-93 (prefixed Catalogue).
Magazine, book, and exhibition titles are given in italics.